Robert Dodsley

Pranceriana

A select collection of fugitive pieces, published since the appointment of the present provost of the University of Dublin

Robert Dodsley

Pranceriana

A select collection of fugitive pieces, published since the appointment of the present provost of the University of Dublin

ISBN/EAN: 9783337218164

Printed in Europe, USA, Canada, Australia, Japan

Cover: Foto ©ninafisch / pixelio.de

More available books at **www.hansebooks.com**

PRANCERIANA.

A SELECT COLLECTION

OF

FUGITIVE PIECES,

PUBLISHED SINCE THE

APPOINTMENT

OF THE

PRESENT PROVOST

OF THE

UNIVERSITY OF DUBLIN.

*Noxia mille modis lacerabitur umbra; tuasque
Æacus in pœnas ingeniosus erit.
In te transcribet veterum tormenta reorum;
Manibus antiquis causa quietis eris.* OVID.

DUBLIN:
MDCCLXXV.

TO THE RIGHT HON.
J——N H————Y H————N,
DOCTOR OF LAWS,

P. T. C.

LATE MAJOR IN THE FOURTH REGIMENT OF HORSE;

REPRESENTATIVE IN THE LATE AND PRESENT PARLIAMENT OF THE CITY OF CORKE;

ONE OF HIS MAJESTY'S COUNCIL AT LAW;

REVERSIONARY REMEMBRANCER OF THE EXCHEQUER;

REVERSIONARY SECRETARY OF STATE;

ONE OF HIS MAJESTY'S MOST HONOURABLE PRIVY COUNCIL;

AND SEARCHER, PACKER, AND GAUGER OF THE PORT OF STRANGFORD.

MY DEAR FRIEND AND COUNTRYMAN,

I HAVE so often told you how much I admired the versatility of your genius and the multiplicity of your pursuits, that it is unnecessary neceffary for me to trouble you, in the ufual ftyle of dedications, with a fulfome eulogium on your character.—Even *Envy*, when fhe reads the motley lift at the head of this dedication, muft own that HARLEQUIN or PROTEUS never underwent fo many metamorphofes as you have done.—Having thus, therefore, immortalized your literary, fenatorial, forenfick, military, and commercial abilities, by erecting to your glory a pillar more durable than brafs, decorated with a fhort but *fignificant* infcription, I fhall proceed at once to that bufinefs which is the occafion of my thus publickly addreffing you.

As *we* have had fo greatly the advantage in the late literary contefts in the univerfity over which you now fo *worthily* prefide, I thought I could not do a more acceptable fervice both to you and to the great fociety to which I belong, than to collect into one view the fugitive pieces that have iffued from the prefs, fince you did us the honour to come among us. We fhall damn our adverfaries to ever-

DEDICATION.

everlasting fame, by thus perpetuating their wretched productions.

With respect to myself I scorn to steal a wreath from any man's brow in order to adorn my own; and therefore beg leave to inform the publick that I am not answerable for any of the pieces in this collection, except those signed with my own name or that of EUSEBIUS. It is quite unnecessary to tell them that all those with the signature of MODERATOR, and THE ACCOUNT of the new Collegiate Regulations, are yours. Your style is marked by such *particularities,* so distinguished by certain *graces* beyond the reach of art, that every *freshman* is now perfectly acquainted with it.—I have taken care to print my famous *dilemma* in capitals, as it is the great bulwark of our cause, and as you have been so kind as to say (pardon my pleasantry) that it is the most *capital* piece of dialecticks that has appeared since the celebrated dilemma of *Protagoras,* recorded by *Aulus Gellius.*

DEDICATION.

It gives me inexpreffible pleafure to think that we fhall thus go down together to pofterity, and to have this opportunity of affuring you that I am, Excellent Sir!

The humbleft, and moft

Obfequious of your vaffals,

NATHAN BEN SADDI.

CONTENTS.

No. 1. TO the *Fellows* and *Scholars* of the university of Dublin.

2. A congratulatory addreſs to the Provoſt, ſigned JUVENIS, by order of the whole body.

3. MODERATOR to the Publick—He vindicates his conduct.

4. VERAX to the Publick, in anſwer to the foregoing Addreſs.

5. A Friend to independence—States the conduct and arguments of Dr. DILEMMA.

6. EUSEBIUS to the PRINTER of the FREEMAN's JOURNAL—Vindicates his friend Dr. DILEMMA.

7. STULTIFEX to EUSEBIUS— Criticiſm on that writer.

8. A FATHER—to the Rev. W. H.———On the duty of a College Tutor.

9. The ſame ſubject continued.

10. PHILODIDACTOR—to the ſcholars of the houſe—States the conduct of the Provoſt, and his agents, with reſpect to the approaching general election.

11. From

CONTENTS.

No. 11. From the same to the same.
12. The same subject continued.
13. NATHAN BEN SADDI to the Printer of the Hibernian Journal—Confesses himself agent to the Provost—Vindicates his own conduct.
14. A *Scholar* of the *House* to the Rev. Mr. *Torrens*—Warns him not to forfeit the esteem of the *Scholars*, by supporting *Black Phil* at the ensuing election.
15. HEROICK EPISTLE from BIDDY FITZPATRICK to WILLIAM DOYLE, Esq;
16. CHARIDEMUS to HIPPARCHUS—on his general character and late promotion.
17. THE VOTE-TRAP; or, a new art of *electioneering*—Dialogue between PRANCERO and Dr. POMPOSO—New rules for speaking in parliament—Epigram on dancing being permitted in the College.
18. MODERATOR's second address to the Publick.
19. ANTI-MODERATOR's remarks on the foregoing address.
20. MODERATOR's third address to the Publick.
21. MODERATOR—to his respectable constituents in the CITY of CORKE.
22. From the same to the same.

23. The

CONTENTS. ix

No. 23. The eleventh ode of the second book of HORACE *imitated*——to Sir John Blaquiere.

24. CHARIDEMUS to HIPPARCHUS——Recommends moderation, and a less *direct* attack on the rights of his people.

25. ANNUS MIRABILIS—The prize poem for 1775.

26. The *Provost*'s ACCOUNT of the regulations made since his appointment.

27. STULTIFEX ACADEMICUS—to the Students of the UNIVERSITY—Criticism on the foregoing ACCOUNT.

28. OLD SLYBOOTS to the Printer of the HIBERNIAN JOURNAL. The same subject continued.

29. History of Mrs. COLLEGE.

30. MARTINUS SCHOLASTICUS to the Printer of the HIBERNIAN JOURNAL—Vindicates the *Provost*'s ACCOUNT of his regulations.

31. CHARIDEMUS to HIPPARCHUS—on duelling—When excuseable—Indefensible in the governor of a learned city.

32. MC BREACHER'S DECREE.

33. CHARIDEMUS to HIPPARCHUS.—Review of his conduct.

34. From

No. 34. From the same to the same. Exhorts the electors of the College to unanimity and firmness.—Account of an outrage committed on a popular Printer.

35. CHARIDEMUS to the CITIZENS of DUBLIN—Exhorts them to shew a proper resentment at the outrage offered to the whole body, in the person of one of their fellow citizens.

36. CHARIDEMUS to VERRES—History of the outrage offered to Mr. Mills—Conduct of Hipparchus with respect to it.

37. FAMILIAR EPISTLE from G—— E—— H————, Esq; to the right hon. J—— H—— H————.

38. Fragments of the memoirs of Mrs. College.

PRANCERIANA.

No. 1.   Saturday, September 3, 1774.

Quos tibi Fortuna ludos facis? Facis enim ex professoribus senatores, ex senatoribus professores.
PLIN. EPIST.

TO THE FELLOWS AND SCHOLARS OF TRINITY-COLLEGE.

* IF the motives which might draw you aside from your duty were extremely forcible, if there were no eyes upon your conduct except your own, if the trust reposed in you were less sacred, if your resentment had been awakened by a slighter indignity than that which you have so lately suffered, I should still expect that you would act as should

---

* It is observable that the late Dr. Andrews was the first instance of the Provost of the University of Dublin obtaining a seat in the House of Commons, as Mr. Hutchinson is the first example of a member of parliament being appointed Provost of that University.—But we find from Juvenal as well as Pliny, that there is nothing new under the sun.

Si Fortuna volet, fies de rhetore consul,
Si volet hæc eadem, fies de consule rhetor.

should become you. You will soon be called upon to decide whether a man, with whom a connection or an intimacy would lately have been a condemnation, has become, by any change of circumstance, a fit person to nominate your representatives. If your *alma mater* has derived any advantage or dignity from his appointment, if his own publick conduct will justify your credulity in those whom he may recommend, you will reward his disinterested attention to your concerns, you will shew every respect to the choice of a chief governor, to whom nothing has appeared so important as the education of the youth of Ireland. But if your society has been conspicuously insulted; if the slightest ministerial arrangement has been preferred to your honour, to your interests, and to the virtues of posterity; if your right of returning members to parliament has been amongst the foremost inducements to this outrage against your privileges; will it be very sanguine in this nation to expect that *you* will not be accessary to the ruin of Irish literature, that you will not ensure future injuries to your society by a gratitude for the past? A government borough so readily corrupted, will never be intrusted to any but the most confidential hands. The motives to such a corruption are almost beneath computation. Who are so independent as the fellows? The scholars of the house neither owe their appointments to Mr. Hutchinson's partiality, nor hold them by his favour. To a transgressing individual his severity may be formidable; against your united indignation, his malice would be impotent.

potent. What then are those powers by which he is to corrupt the young, and to frighten the independent? Powers of injuring, which women would despise; powers of rewarding, by which a Cornish borough would not be corrupted. Without any connection except that of the undoer with the undone, Mr. Hutchinson expects to dictate to you, where the constitution has made you free. Two months ago, a political recantation would hardly have procured him toleration amongst you. You are now to consider how a new crime can recommend him.

If, contrary to the just expectations of the public, to gratitude, and to the trust reposed in you, you should betray the interests of that society which supports you, be not ignorant that all other infamy would be obliterated by yours. Not the miserable mechanick who throws away that constitution which he knows not how to estimate, not the poor, the ignorant, the flattered, or the deceived elector, but the learned, the independent, the young, the injured will monopolize the publick indignation—men will then say, it is not Harcourt, it is not Hutchinson that has undone our university—but its own guardians—Not the general who corrupts the garrison but the soldier who betrays it, is the most infamous of men.—Lord Harcourt gave them but one Hutchinson; all his successors who shall resemble him are appointed—by the servility of Trinity College. That slight estimation in which he held them, and in which he was not mistaken, rather does credit to his capacity—For it is certain, that very few at that time, knew them so well. Rather let every father return him thanks for having made known the true character of our University. The body, which in such circumstances, could reject an *Hussey*, never can produce another*.

※※※※※※※※※※※※※※※※※※※※※※※※

No. 2.   *Wednesday, November* 16, 1774.

> *Diu*
> *Lateque victrices catervæ*
> *Consiliis* JUVENIS *revictæ*
> *Sensere quid mens rite, quid indoles*
> *Nutrita faustis sub penetralibus*
> *Posset.*   HOR.

An ADDRESS *to the Right Honoured and most learned* JOHN HELY HUTCHINSON, *Esq; Provost of the College of the Holy and Undivided Trinity, near Dublin.*

WE your Provostship's most dutiful and loyal pupils, the students of Trinity College, Dublin, do most humbly presume to approach your presence, and congratulate you on your elevation to the station of Provost of this College, which your surprising knowledge in every branch of human erudition has so wonderfully qualified you for.

With

---

* Since the writing of the above, the independent electors of the university have nominated Walter Hussey and Edmond Malone, Esqrs. as proper persons to represent them in the ensuing parliament.

With admiration we behold a person of your honourable and reputable extraction, incorruptible integrity, nervous eloquence, and gracefulness of person; in short, a being possessed of so many rare endowments of body and mind, that though it be impossible to pronounce in which of these you excel, yet the one serves to add the greater brilliancy to the other; placed as you now are at the head of a society which may, if not viewed in the blaze of your perfections, be called learned; and we congratulate ourselves that we happen to be members of the university at a time, when you, who are the *Decus et Columen Patriæ*, are wisely placed as a crutch to support our *Alma Mater*, tottering under infirmities from internal disorders.

How do our breasts swell with gratitude to the discerning and gracious Harcourt, and his sagacious secretary, Sir John Blaquiere? To these excellent judges of literary merit, did you wisely and happily for this seminary, display your knowledge of *Thucydides* and *Demosthenes peri Stephanou*; convinced them, (and easily they were convinced,—such is the force of your oratory) that *Scaliger* and *Casaubon* were but novices to you; and that passages which were to these critics inexplicable, easily yielded up their hitherto hidden treasures to your all-subduing sagacity, and were even known to your illustrious progeny *a Cunabulis*, by intuition: Hence this delegate and sub-delegate of Majesty, subdued by the incessant repetition of *Thucydides*, and *Demosthenes peri Stephanou*, as the moon by the incantations of *Circe*, easily yielded to your desires, and constituted you Provost merely for the emolument of the *Respublica Literaria*.

With shame we must confess, that none of our present *fellows* were equal to the arduous task of governing this college, and promoting the study of the fine arts. Drones as they are, which of them was qualified to be professor of equestrian exercises? The institution of that illustrious professorship was reserved to grace the æra of your government. Professors of dancing, fencing, &c. we may expect from your unwearied endeavours to promote the interest of this great seminary, and to render us all humble, though distant imitators of your most graceful deportment.

Permit us to assure you, most learned Sir, as your promotion has been so much owing to your intimate acquaintance with, and repetition of these cabalistical expressions, *Thucydides* and *Demosthenes peri Stephanou*; that every man of us will incessantly repeat those words, in humble imitation of your profound learning, of which they have been, as it were, the test, seal and mark, in the presence of every great man whom we may occasionally be in company with; and that we shall most carefully practise and encourage the art of harmoniously *haranguing upon nothing*, of which useful science you daily prove yourself a compleat master, as well in the senate as at the bar, in both places speaking for hours, nay whole days together, without uttering one

one argument of which the most acute senator or barrister can take hold.

Suffer us then, *Potosi* of erudition, humbly to lay ourselves at your feet, and implore your protection, and to assure you, that when a period shall be put to this present parliament, we will all chearfully concur in electing for members, to represent this university, such persons as you shall condescend to nominate; firmly relying, that you will dictate to our choice, for that important trust, persons only, who will be as disinterested as yourself, and though not equal to you in learning, (a thing in its nature impossible,) yet as learned as you can procure, and such as have been educated in that nurse of genius, the illustrious college of Eton, near Windsor; whose lively imaginations have not been sullied by the laborious study of philosophy, which to the disgrace of all true gentleman-like education, is yet permitted to dwell within this college; but which we hope soon to see totally expelled, under your auspices, by preceptors in horsemanship, fencers, dancers, and musicians: and we also presume to assure *your learned eminence*, that we shall, on all other occasions be your *most humble slaves*; to convince every future chief governor, that no member of this university ought to be taken notice of by his Majesty's servants, on a future vacancy of the provostship, (which heaven for a long term of years avert! *Serus in Cælum redeas!*) but that persons equally well skilled with *your eminence*, in all kind of parliamentary

liamentary service to the crown, are the only persons qualified to superintend the education of the youth of this happy and flourishing kingdom.

(Signed by order of the rest)

JUVENIS.

No. 3.   *Monday, November 28, 1774.*

Quos ego—sed motos prestat componere fluctus.   VIRG.

To the PUBLICK.

MANY attempts having been lately made to influence the minds of the Scholars, directly tending to the subversion of all discipline and subordination in the University, for preventing those ruinous consequences, it is become necessary to state to the public the truth of the transaction which has been made the pretext for much misrepresentation:

On Wednesday the 9th instant, at two o'clock, the head porter of the College brought the Provost a paper, which had been posted that day upon the great gate of the chapel, in the words following: " The electors of the College are requested to meet
" this

" this day at two o'clock, at Ryan's in Fownes's-
" street, to consider of proper persons to be put in
" nomination as candidates for this University at the
" ensuing general election." The Provost did not
enter into the occasion of this meeting, but considered the posting of a notice in the College for the assembling of the Scholars at a tavern, as a dangerous innovation, and as an example of the most pernicious tendency to the tranquility, and good government of the College; and, therefore, sent the two deans to inform the young gentlemen assembled, that he did not enter into the subject of their meeting, but ordered them to disperse, and retire to their rooms; they at first refused, but the Provost having again sent the two deans to them to warn them of the fatal consequences of their disobedience, they dispersed. On the next day the Provost thought it his duty to consult the Senior Fellows upon this occasion, and having recommended the most gentle mode of proceeding that could be thought of, referred the decision to them, and with their concurrence, and in their presence reproved the Scholars who had assembled, in the following words:

" Gentlemen Scholars of the House,

" In consequence of the unanimous opinion of
" this board, I am to reprove you for your assembling
" yesterday at Ryan's tavern, as such meetings tend
" to the subversion of discipline, the disturbance of
" the peace, and the interruption of the studies of
" the

" the College; and also for your refusal to disperse,
" and retire to your rooms, when the Provost sent
" the two deans to you with his orders to that pur-
" pose: and I am happy that your dispersing after
" receiving a second order from the Provost, has
" put it in the power of the board to avoid inflict-
" ing a severer punishment than this reproof, which
" I give you in the performance of my duty; and
" the board hope you will have a just sense of their
" lenity upon this occasion, and expect that this
" will be a sufficient caution to you not to repeat
" those offences for the future."

The power of the Scholars to meet for nominating candidates was never considered, nor was it necessary or proper to be considered by the Provost or the board; but the Provost in dispersing, and the board in reproving, did not in any respect interfere with the design of their meeting, but acted only with a view to the discipline of the college.

The dispersing the assembly of Wednesday the 9th instant, could have answered no election purpose; the impracticability of preventing the Scholars of the house, if so disposed, from associating or nominating candidates, is obvious; and enforcing the discipline of the College in this instance against *those* gentlemen, as students, must have offended them as electors; but, a meeting of the Scholars at a tavern, in Term time, and in consequence of a notice posted in the College for that purpose, is a transaction faction unheard of in any University, and would have been subversive of all order in this, if the Provost had not interposed, after having received official information of it.

The electors of the College have the same rights with all other electors; *those* rights have never been questioned, and the fullest exercise of them is perfectly consistent with the preservation of good order in the College. But, it should be remembered that the Scholars of the house are students as well as electors; that they are all of them very young men, and several of them under age; that some of them will cease to be electors before a vacancy shall happen, and others will not then have that capacity from being minors; and that, if the subject of election, when there is no vacancy, shall be considered as a sufficient reason for the Scholars assembling in town whenever they shall think proper, they may do so at any time or times, from one parliament to another, and the power of the Provost and Fellows to keep them in the College, upon which the whole system of discipline principally depends, will be entirely subverted.

Let experience be appealed to, and it will be found, that there has never been an instance of such a meeting, when there was no vacancy, either in this or any other college.

The senior fellows have unanimously censured this meeting, as tending to subvert the discipline, disturb the peace, and interrupt the studies of the college. *Those* gentlemen are of known ability and integrity; have been for many years conversant in the government of this university, and cannot be supposed to have been influenced by any other motives than the general good of the society.

If any thing oppressive or arbitrary should be attempted in this university, the publick has a right to animadvert; but if in mere matters of discipline there is to be an appeal to the publick, from the unanimous determination of the provost and senior fellows, the government of this great and numerous society will become impracticable.

The statutes of the college oblige the scholars to obey the provost in all matters of discipline. The scholars of the house are sworn to obey the statutes, and to obey the provost in all things honest and lawful, with the readiest will and zeal; and consequently are bound to follow his directions in all matters of discipline, which the provost may, in all cases, not expressly provided for by the statutes, either determine himself or refer to the board; the latter method was upon this occasion adopted, as the most moderate, and the least liable to misrepresentation.

The

The only objection to the best disciplined, and one of the most learned universities in the world, is its situation in a metropolis. Great pains have been taken to guard against this inconvenience, by not permitting the students to resort to the city, but under certain restrictions. If the scholars of the house shall be allowed to assemble in the city in great numbers, and to fix up notices for that purpose, and if the heat and violence of party shall find their way from the city into the college; that objection will alarm every thinking man in this kingdom.

This is not the cause of the provost, or of the senior fellows;—it is the cause of your sons and kinsmen, of the rising generation, and of posterity. Allay *those* ferments; suffer not the peace of this society to be longer disturbed;—and do not render it impossible for the provost and fellows to do their duty by your own children.

From this true state of facts, every man of discernment must see that the dispersing this meeting was calculated solely for the welfare and tranquility of the students, and could have had no possible view of restraining their liberty, or influencing their votes; and that a connivance at such a meeting, though it might have flattered the young gentlemen, would have been criminal in the governor of a college, who, in this instance, sacrificed every view of election policy to the faithful and disinterested performance of his duty.

MODERATOR.

No. 4.   *Monday, December 5, 1774.*

Εχθρὸς γὰρ μοι κεῖνος ὁμῶς ἀϊδαο πύλησιν
Ὅς χέτερον μὲν κεύθει ἐνὶ φρεσὶν ἄλλο δὲ βάζει.

Who dares think one thing and another tell,
My heart detests him as the gates of hell.

TO THE PRINTER OF THE HIBERNIAN JOURNAL:

AN addreſs to the publick, ſigned, *Moderator*, appeared in your Journal of the 28th of November laſt; which, from the length and inanity of its periods and arguments, and its ſtudied mixture of falſhood and truth, may, with the greateſt probability, be concluded to have been the production of the pen of our provoſt; and as the public may be miſled by this addreſs, and the jobbing, the petulance, ignorance, and incapacity for his employment of this little intruder, paſs on the uninformed public as zeal for the welfare of this unfortunate ſeminary, if the untruths and miſrepreſentations contained in it were to continue unveiled, I have thought proper to mark the ſeveral falſhoods, and miſrepreſentations of this piece, in their order; at the ſame time aſſuring the publick, that I have had the beſt information of every tranſaction relative to the meeting of the ſcholars of the college

college on the 9th of November; their arbitrary and unwarrantable dispersion; and the proceedings of the provost and board thereon: and that tho' I heartily abhor the intruder, and the shameless administration who made him our governor, yet my abhorrence shall not cause me to swerve from the strictest truth.

First, the provost insinuates, that, " he gained " his intelligence of this meeting of the scholars, " at two o'clock on the 9th of November, when " the paper mentioned in his address was brought " him by the head porter, officially;" now, I assert, that the fact was not so; but that he had notice of the intended meeting of the scholars on the 8th of Nov. from a mean, warm, weak man in the college, who acts for him in the double capacity of a spy, and an adviser, and by whose intemperate counsels he is wise enough to be chiefly guided in college affairs; and that he determined to leave the Four-courts early on the 9th of Nov. in order to disperse that meeting; which he did accordingly disperse, in the manner he has mentioned: and that on the morning of that day he had given orders to the head porter to watch and bring him any paper which might be posted on the gates of the college.

Next he asserts, that he was influenced to disperse it, from considering " the posting of a no-
" tice in the college for assembliag the scholars at a
" tavern, as a dangerous innovation, and as an ex-
" ample of the most pernicious tendency to the
" tranquillity

"tranquillity and good government of the college;
"and that he did not enter into the occasion of this
"meeting." What a plausible, and at the same
time, most flagrant falshood is this? In order to expose it sufficiently, I must necessarily give an account of the cause of this meeting, and shew that all the present ferment and disorder in the college has originated from the provost himself. A few days before the meeting, the provost sent for all the tutors in the college, and told them he intended at the next general election, to recommend two candidates to the choice of the university, one of whom should be his own son, and requested their votes and interests with their respective pupils, who are scholars of the house. This was received as the very signal for electioneering. Such of the scholars as resented the barbarous treatment the college had received from government, in robbing them of their greatest, and, indeed, the almost only valuable prize they had for literary merit, and bestowing it on a little parliamentary brawler, immediately caught the alarm; and thinking that this was the time to shew their resentment, by asserting their independency, and convincing administration that they would return two members as disagreeable to the court as possible; and that they might, perhaps, by this measure, secure the reversion of the provostship to the college, agreed that it would be proper to have a meeting for the purpose of nominating two candidates; and accordingly the paper mentioned in the provost's address, was posted on the gate of

the

the chapel. The provoſt getting intelligence of this intended meeting at the time, and from the perſon before mentioned, determined to diſperſe it, from the ſole motive of preventing the ſcholars from nominating two candidates contrary to his intereſt, and not from any of the motives mentioned in his addreſs: of this any perſon may be convinced who will conſider the following circumſtances.—Firſt, I am well informed, that he himſelf told the board, which he aſſembled on this affair, that he had notice of this meeting the day before it was held; and that he came home early on the 9th of Nov. from the Four-courts, in order to diſperſe it, and had given the aforementioned order to the head porter; ſo that he would have diſperſed them in the ſame manner, if the notice had not been poſted: the poſting of the notice, therefore, was no part of his motives for diſperſing the meeting, as he aſſerts. Secondly, The meeting of the ſcholars at a tavern, on ſuch an occaſion, was not contrary to any of the ſtatutes of the college, and therefore he had no right whatſoever to take ſuch notice of it. The frequenting of taverns is forbidden by the ſtatutes with a view to the preſervation of ſobriety and order; but going once to a tavern, on ſuch a ſerious and ſolemn occaſion, and before dinner, at which time there was no danger of intemperance, can never be called frequenting taverns in the ſtatutable ſenſe, or in any ſenſe whatſoever; and therefore his diſperſing them could not ariſe from any view to the good government of the college, which is ſufficiently provided for by the

ſtatutes,

statutes, and does not stand in need of any absurd new regulations of such a provost, which may be justly called innovations —Thirdly, If it should be granted that such meetings tend to the disturbance of the tranquillity of the college, yet in this case it must also be granted, that the provost himself made that meeting necessary, by first commencing his operations in electioneering; and that therefore he was the disturber of the tranquillity of the college. —Fourthly, His indiscreet, hasty, ill-judged behaviour throughout the whole transaction, together with his petulant and impotent menaces to the junior dean*, shew his real design in dispersing the meeting, and that preservation of order and discipline was no part of it.

In the next place he asserts, that " he thought " it his duty to consult the fellows on this occasion, " and having recommended the most gentle mode " of proceeding that could be thought of, referred " the decision to them." Very condescending, indeed! The truth of this matter stands thus :—The provost was extremely desirous to punish some of the leading scholars for their no crime in assembling, and afterwards dispersing on his order, and finding the statutes did not give him any power to inflict a punishment by his own authority (the provost's sole authority of punishing without the board being limited to certain crimes specified in the statutes) he assembled a board, and I am well informed that he was so far from recommending the most gentle mode of

* Mr. R—d—n.

of proceeding, that he endeavoured, by his pretty perfuasive oratory, to induce the fellows to rusticate three or four of the leading scholars, which is the next punishment to expulsion; but, finding he was seconded in this by none but Didymus* (the sycophant of living, and Calumniator of dead provosts) he was obliged to drop it, and content himself with reproving them, in the manner set forth in his address; at the same time, in the rage of his disappointment, declaring to the board, that if these scholars (twenty-four in number, and the flower of the university with respect to learning and morals) had not dispersed at his second sending to them, he would have expelled them all, by his own authority, for contumacy.—Rare instance of his understanding and mildness!

He next asserts, " That there never has been an " instance of such a meeting, when there was no " vacancy, either in this, or any other college." To this it may be answered, very truly, that this is the first time any provost of this college has begun to electioneer before a vacancy, and therefore the meeting of the electors became necessary, to counteract his operations, before the vacancy.

His next assertion contains a doctrine never heard of in the college, " that the provost may in all cases, " not expressly provided for by the statutes, either " determine himself, or refer to the board." I say he cannot in any case whatsoever, not expressly provided

* Dr. L———d.

vided for by the statutes, determine himself, but must and ought to refer to the board, in all such cases; and therefore in this transaction he did not refer to the board, as thinking such reference *"the most moderate method, and the least liable to misrepresentation;"* but he referred to the board, for the reasons I have before fully mentioned His supplication to the public, towards the close of his ad'ress, is really ludicrous: " Allay these ferments; suffer " not the peace of this society to be longer disturbed, " and do not render it impossible for the provost " and fellows to do their duty by your own chil-" dren." That is, this incendiary has set a house on fire, and then, to avoid suspicion, calls for the parish engine. What does he mean by doing his duty to the students in the college? The most galling part of the injury done us by making him provost is, that his petulance, if possible, exceeds his ignorance, and that in consequence of both, he is every day insulting us by his pretences to knowledge, and by proposing absurd, crude and impracticable regulations, both in discipline and instruction; and certain I am, that his appointment to his present station, *has alarmed every thinking man in this kingdom.*

Thus I have gone through this famous address, and hope that I have sufficiently exposed the misrepresentations contained in it; and I solemnly aver, that I have been influenced to this publication by no other views but the love of truth, and my hatred

tred of all those vipers who sacrifice every thing that ought to be dear to a citizen, to their inordinate desire of power and riches, and will boldly grasp at every employment, sacred or profane, provided it is a lucrative one, let them be ever so unfit for it, and though their notorious incapacity should bring ruin on their country.

VERAX.

No. 5.   *Tuesday, December 6, 1774.*

TO THE REV. D———R F———S———TH, J—N—R D—N OF T———TY C———GE.

IF your conduct had been only contemptible, I should not have troubled you with this publick address. If you had continued to pay the meanest adulations to bishops and other men in power, and had not attempted to corrupt the hearts and destroy the principles of the youth of this university, I should have suffered your infamy to be confined to these walls, and not have published your character to the world. I mean not to mention a single point, the truth of which is not incontestable; many I shall even suppress: for if I was to recount the numerous absurdities and vile practises you have
been

been guilty of, I should swell this letter to the size of a volume. When Dr. Andrews was provost, no man talked more loudly than you of the propriety of opposing his dictates, and of the necessity that men of liberal educations should convince the world of the liberality of their sentiments, and give the kingdom an example of disinterested independence. But your behaviour since a late promotion, has evinced, that it was the man alone you opposed. How consistent does it appear in the person, who, on the last college election, asserted he would have gone to the publick meetings of the scholars, if he could have found a single fellow to accompany him: how consistent, I say, does it appear in such a man to declare, only because the head of this society is changed, that they acted not only contrary to law, but contrary to their oaths, who lately assembled to fix on such candidates as would, by their integrity and abilities, reflect the highest honour on their choice? You, sir, are undoubtedly a man of learning, yet have been hurried on by your intemperance to treat men of learning as if they were fools: for had you not considered them as fools, you would never have supported the cause you have espoused with absurd arguments and futile dilemmas. That the publick may be acquainted with your reasonings on this subject, I shall mention *that* one, on which you seem to lay a particular stress. You assert, THAT IF THE PROVOST IS A GOOD MAN HE OUGHT NOT TO BE OPPOSED; IF A BAD MAN, THAT OPPOSITION WOULD BE FRUITLESS; for he could nominate

nominate two classes of scholars before the election, which would secure him a majority of voices.

I hope there is not at present a gentleman in the university who would accept of a scholarship on such terms; and I will do Mr. Hutchinson the justice to say, I believe he never once entertained so wicked an idea. I doubt not, sir, if *you* were provost, you would execute what you have conceived. I doubt not but you would attempt every act of injustice in your own cause, when you have gone such lengths to support another's. When our present provost was appointed, he did not pretend to be acquainted with our interests. By your advice he is constantly directed; by your advice he arbitrarily dispersed the free electors; and to your advice must be attributed that daring impropriety which has already discovered itself in the whole of his conduct. I blame him not for his misdeeds. When appointed, thanks to the *wisdom* and *goodness* of our chief governor, he knew nothing of the duty of his office; he relied entirely on you for information, and you misled him.' For the precipitancy and intemperance which makes so considerable a part of your character, are sufficiently marked in that arbitrary and peevish system of government which every occurrence gives us occasion to see he has adopted; and for the execution of which it is notorious that you have been appointed *dean*, irregularly, and out of the due course in which that office should go among the junior fellows. Some
few

few circumstances more of your conduct I shall remind you of, and conclude. You had the insolence to charge some scholars with ingratitude, for not avowing slavish principles; because, through your means, they had obtained from the provost and board what *they* considered as *the reward of merit*, and *you*, as your treatment of them evinces, *a bribe*. You had the baseness to misrepresent the conduct of others to their parents; and you had the meanness to sue for the office you enjoy, in order to possess the power of oppressing, with the appearance of justice, every independent scholar of the college. This, sir, is the first time you have ever heard from me, I assure you it shall be the last. I shall consider you for the future as sunk below my notice; as unworthy of my pen. It will be fruitless to attempt discovering my name, as I have taken every method to keep it concealed; and your knowing it can be of no consequence, as I am far above the reach of your resentment.

I am, Sir,

A friend to independence,

and a member of this university.

No. 6.

No 6.   *Thursday, December 8, 1774.*

How fluent nonsense trickles from his tongue!
How sweet the periods, neither said, nor sung. POPE.

TO THE PRINTER OF THE FREEMAN'S JOURNAL.

SIR,

ON Tuesday December the 6th, a letter appeared in the Freeman's Journal addressed to our Junior Dean, and subscribed *A Friend to Independence, and a Member of the College.* When an independent spirit assumes the frightful feature of slander unprovoked, shall we acknowledge him a friend to independence? When the production of a distempered brain shall be offered as academical composition, shall his signature be undisputed?

Gentlemen of generous thoughts and liberal education, seldom embark on the ocean of defamation, restrained by humanity and delicacy of sentiment. As it is impossible to explore the variety of motives to action that influence a publick character, mature reflection will often suspend censure, justified even by a combination of appearances; yet poignant reproof and genteel satire, in many circumstances are salutary—are necessary—and the stigmatized infamy of vile assassins, of *character* exalted, should restrain

restrain abandoned inducements to groundless calumny. The sluices of honest indignation, drawn in virtue's defence, should overwhelm in oblivion the odious enemy of venerated honour.

How could thy poisoned pen, dull son of Scriblerus, dare address the idol of publick applause in the language of scurrility. The conspicuous object of general acclamation, thy baleful hissing cannot effect nor disturb. By the native dignity of a regulated temper secured, at thy impotence, thy envenomed scandal he smiles. Thy utmost efforts, exerted in an inferior sphere, can never reach a breast unconscious of guilt. Possessed of our affectionate obedience, he proceeds in that distinguished course, which has already attracted publick attention. Possessed of activity which no toil can conquer, his endeavours are directed to restore to the university ancient discipline, dignity and erudition.

Secular concerns and fashionable amusements, engaged many in a course of life inconsistent with their appointments. Hence ideas prejudicial to the seminary were generally adopted: and a reformation became a matter of serious attention. In this state was the college incontestibly immersed, and lovers of this country felt sensible affliction. However the dean attempted a renovation, and may the genius of Ireland smile on his efforts. Wherever council can operate, he is ever ready to
reclaim.

reclaim. When persuasive accents make no impression on dissolute lives, we see him support his character, and enforce the statutes with intrepidity and resolution. Should his aid become necessary in the sciences, to a laborious student, we see him assist, direct with encouraging alacrity. In a word, vigilance to reform, perseverance in design, and humanity to relieve, are the outlines of this character.

Though the exertions of such an active spirit command admiration, the infectious eye of zealous predecessors in office, cannot endure that superiority which exposes their indolence. An irregular being, at once a disgrace to the college, and a scandal to his family, who could never yield to the *least* controul, cannot brook the severity of regulation. Behold this unfortunate youth, in society of equal perverseness, declaim against dean, literature, parentage, nay heaven itself! That reflection may cure their obstinacy, ere dissipation consumes their intellects and fortune, is assuredly the wish of the doctor, to which all his labours are directed.

I cannot persuade myself, that the scandal alluded to was written by a student; but, by supposing it the undigested essay of one of those clamorous spirits—still this conjecture is improbable—And indeed it is a subject I should discuss with no other design than to exculpate *gentlemen* from the odium a foul infinuation, viz. That a futile letter, inelegant as it is fcandalous, fhould be written by one of their body, traducing the beft of men. This *would-be* member of our univerfity, introduces a fyftem of reafoning as the doctor's, that would difgrace an ideot ; and has effrontery to expect credit to fuch forged affertions : but it is well known, that the doctor fhines in converfation, as in writing: he is cool and attentive—of engaging fweetnefs. Diffidence in his own, and profound deference to the opinion of others, fecure him fuperiority in the moft learned circles ; and all this accompanied with nervous fenfe and dignity of expreffion. I would not be underftood to give the world an inadequate idea of this great man—from inability. I only give a feint tranfcript of my own feelings ;—but finding even this difficult, a fact which I fhall relate to the world, will fpeak for me, and apologize, I hope, for my own emotions, and pleafe the benevolent.

A poor daughter of affliction, who had feen happy days, lay wafted on the bed of woe, by the combined preffure of infirmity and want—on the pillow of difeafe and care lay this parent of fix children for the fpace of fourteen months. All fuccours from a few friends, and the charitable within the circle of her acquaintance, being exhaufted, fhe pined with acute pain, and the yearnings of a mother for poor orphans ! Deftitute, cold, and hungry ! An old woman attending in this college vifited the melancholy fcene, and fympathized !
—who,

—who, having learned an additional stroke to the plaintive tale, and paid nature the tribute of a tear, said she was sure Doctor Forsayeth would gladly succour them, were half their sufferings explained to him. On hearing this the eldest child, eleven years of age, stole out unperceived, ran to the college, and fortunately met the doctor.——On her knees she unfolded her heart in three words, more emphatically than the learned could do, perhaps, in so many volumes: " my mother is starving, and will not live 'till to-morrow." Some circumstances making it impossible to get any sort of a carriage, he walked a considerable distance, of a cold night at eleven o'clock, to convert the house of mourning into joy—to alleviate the sorrows of a broken heart! Hear how he succeeded: the mother is now an upper servant in a family of distinction, and her children at trade. Adept in the most infernal rancour, digest this anecdote and repent of thy sacrilege.

An explanation of the doctor's connection with the present, and his opposition to the late provost, may be the subject of another epistle. And if I shall be able to demonstrate the uniformity of conduct, the unchangeable tenor and consistency of his life, gentlemen, too preciptate in decision, will, I hope, take reflection for their guide. These observations arise from sentiments which his piety and many amiable qualities have inspired, and are published as a duty incumbent on every student, in testimony of his abhorrence of that audacious attempt to asperse the established reputation of a worthy man. Let it not be imagined that this letter is a compliment, in consequence of an intimacy or interested hope,—no, I am totally disengaged from influencing attachments, endeavouring to vindicate merit from the vile effusions of malice and gross misrepresentation.

Unawed by human resentment, I should exhibit to publick animadversion the most dignified villain, when his principles interfered with the constitutional happiness of my native country: but it seems that far different motives sway the heart of this scribbling mortal, who introduces to publick view an illiberal attack, without the slightest foundation—an impeachment indeed unheard, unprecedented. Vainly imagining, that he had given a mortal stab, he ludicrously asserts the impossibility of discovering his retreat,—equally obscure as his stile. Go, son of darkness and nocturnal infamy—go—immure thyself and accursed machinations, in dreary wilderness, estranged for ever from that society which thy *heart* could injure, and never more provoke the pen of

EUSEBIUS.

No. 7.

No. 7.   *Saturday, December* 10, 1774.

And he who now to sense, now nonsense leaning,
Means not, but blunders round about a meaning.
POPE.

TO EUSEBIUS.

MASTER Eusebius! master Eusebius! check your nag for one moment, I beseech you. For God's sake, man, use your bone-setter a little gently on the high road of common sense.— Here am I quite out of breath, dashing after you this half hour through all the bye-paths of old Farnaby and Smiglecius——But enough of metaphor.

Two whole columns (in answer to a *particular* charge) of such *inanities* as these!

  D—r F—yth "is the idol of publick ap-
     "plause."
    "the conspicuous object of ge-
     "neral acclamation."
    "he shines in conversation as in
     "writing."
    "he is cool and attentive."

"he is of engaging sweetness."
"he is a great man!"

And eighthly and lastly, he relieved a poor old woman after "her daughter had, on her knees, un-"folded her—story to him!" What a vindicator!

But as if this dose of fulsome impertinence were not enough to sicken the publick, you must choak them with absurdities. Mark this:

"When an *independent* spirit assumes the fright-"ful feature of slander unprovoked, shall we ac-"knowledge him a friend to independence?"

Is it *secundum Smiglecium* to predicate absolutely of your subject, in the beginning of a letter, what you intend to deny in the end?

Mark again:

"Thy utmost efforts, *exerted in an inferior* "*sphere*, can never reach a breast unconscious of "guilt."

So that were they exerted in a *superior sphere*, we may infer that they might reach such a breast. Excellent panegyrick!

You may perhaps imagine, *Eusebius*, that I know you, that I am your enemy, or the enemy of of the cause you espouse.—It is a mistake; I neither know you, nor have a wish against you or d—r F——yth; but I have an irreconcileable aversion to turgid verbosity, to inflated nonsense, especially from TRIN. COLL. the chaste mother, I would hope, of simplicity and dignity.

Let me appeal to yourself, Eusebius, whether any querulous attorney's clerk, who had been whipt through Sallust, could put a *plain thought* in a more pedantick dress than this:

"As it is impossible to explore the variety of mo-
"tives to action that influence a publick character,
"mature reflection will often suspend censure, jus-
"tified even by a combination of appearances; yet
"poignant reproof and gentle satire, in many cir-
"cumstances are salutary—are necessary—and the
"stigmatized infamy of vile assassins, of character
"*exalted*, should restrain abandoned inducements to
"groundless calumny. The sluices of honest in-
"dignation, drawn in virtue's defence, should
"overwhelm in oblivion the odious enemy of ve-
"nerated honour."

In English thus, if I do not mistake the meaning.

Mature reflection will often induce us to suspend our censure of a publick character, however striking the appearances, because it will inform as how

difficult

difficult it is to discover the motives to action. It must however be confessed that, poignant reproof and genteel satire, are on many occasions salutary—nay, necessary—but then the infamy which awaits the character of a *traducer*, should deter a man from engaging, at least for a common bribe, in the task of groundless calumny: the burst of universal indignation must overwhelm such a fellow.

You may perceive from this specimen, Eusebius, what is my object. It is, in truth, not whether you or your opponent be right, but whether you shall both tell your story in a manner worthy the publick eye, and that will not disgrace us in a London circle: your adversary wrote, at least, like a man that could write. Had I any other end in view, I would censure particular expressions; such as *the sluices drawn*, in the foregoing extract, which is not English.

I always understood that, in proportion as a tale was true or untrue, as it was affecting or otherwise, *decoration* or *painting*, was or was not requisite: but you, who had only to defend an honest man, and to relate a mere fact, (not that your fact is to the purpose) have dissipated your force in superfluous epithet, and unpointed amplification.

There are so many men in Dublin, to my knowledge, better qualified for the task of reviewing than I am, that I beseech you to believe that, nothing

thing less than a sincere love for *Alma Mater* and *my country* could make me sweat you thus, my dear Eusebius!

STULTIFEX.

No. 8. *Tuesday, December* 13, 1774.

Exigite ut mores teneros ceu pollice ducat
Ut si quis cæra vultum facit; exigite ut sit
Et pater ipsius cætus.   Juv.

TO THE REV. W. H. J. F. T. C. D.

SIR,

WHEN I was advised to put my son under your care, the recommendation which principally influenced my choice, was the expectation (industriously suggested to me) " that he would have the benefit too, of being in some measure under the tuition of your friend the Doctor."* Though disappointed in that expectation, I did not complain, while by attending solely to the duty of a Tutor, your diligence made some amends for other deficiencies: for, so excellent is the course in our College, that any lad of common sense and capacity must be a tolerable good scholar, if obliged to attend regularly, and study carefully. But I now see

the

* Dr. *Forsayeth.*

the folly of intrusting the tuition of a boy, to one of as little experience, and as liable to be misled as himself; one whose character and disposition the world is as little acquainted with, as he with the world.

The conduct of your friend has proved him a very unfit person, to be intrusted with the important care of forming the minds of youth. From the first insight into his turn therefore, I little regretted his not taking the share, I was at first persuaded he would, in the education of my son; nor was I much dissatisfied, when I found of late, that you misemployed the time of Lecture, in vindicating the absurdities of the Doctor, instead of unravelling the perplexities of science, or explaining the beauties of the classicks. I excused the abuse of tutelar authority, while exercised only to lighten the weight of publick odium on your friend. But, when you not only quit the line of duty, to deviate into the extravagance of his errors; but even rush into the labyrinth of politicks, in which neither of you ought ever to entangle yourselves; when you descend to the menial officiousness of a time-serving tool; and publickly labour to inculcate slavish principles of non-resistance, and to seduce your pupils into *unmanly submission*; I own my patience is tried to the utmost; and, whatever other parents may think, as I privately condemn, I will publickly upbraid. Your offence is publick; its tendency is of publick import; and it deserves to be made as notorious, as it is dangerous.

Among

Among the many obnoxious tenets, which you (Sir) have exercised all your little influence and art, to prevail on young gentlemen to admit; you even advanced this doctrine, improper at any time, but most preposterous now: "That Scholars of the "House ought not to refuse, to vote for candidates "recommended by the Provost." A position, so false and illiberal, so publickly obtruded upon young minds, demands a publick descant.

Leaving therefore the follies of your friend the Doctor, for the Scholars to ridicule, the Fellows to despise, your imprudence to palliate, and the Provost to countenance and reward; I shall endeavour by refuting you, who first presumed to scatter such dangerous seed, to prevent its taking root in our University. My concern for the rising generation, my love of true learning, my attachment to my country, and my zeal for liberty, will not suffer me to be silent; especially in a matter wherein my own son is so essentially interested. For his sake therefore, and that of the other Scholars, you may expect to hear again from an injured and offended

FATHER.

No, 9.

No. 9.   *Thursday, December* 15, 1774.

Dii Majorum umbris tenuem & fine pondere terram
Spirantesque crocos, et in urna perpetuum ver,
Qui præceptorem sancti voluere parentis
Esse loco.

JUV.

TO THE REV. W. H. J. F. T. C. D.

THERE scarce can be a more convincing proof, that it is criminal and scandalous in a *Provost*, to attempt any bias on the suffrage of a Scholar, than the melancholy instance at the last Election : an instance, which cost a worthy youth his life ; and a man of genius, his honour and repose. What was it, so incensed Doctor ANDREWS against JOHNSON ?' Not his petulance or opposition ; for he overlooked the same in others. No : it was his publickly branding him with the infamous crime, of *tampering* with the Scholars : a crime, Sir, of which ANDREWS could not bear the imputation though You and *your Friend* can bear the guilt of it : a crime, Sir, which (if proved upon the man, for whom You have so harangued the Scholars, and *your*
Friend

Friend has so inflamed them) must disappoint the selfish purposes, for which it is committed. As *Head of the College*, it is disgraceful and unjust in a Provost, to exert any influence on the voters; as *Returning-officer*, it is insolent and penal.

What therefore it is neither lawful nor honest for a Provost, to solicit, it cannot be lawful or honest for a Scholar, to grant. The duty is reciprocal; and the violation of it is alike criminal in both: the corrupter and corrupted alike are guilty. The Rope of the *Pulley* is equally strained, by the weight that is moved, and the power that moves it; and every wheel, in the machine, bears its share of the load. For these reasons I aver, ' the Scholars of the House
' ought not to vote for any Candidate the *Provost*
' recommends:' nay, I aver, ' a Canditate whom *he*
' recommends (how unexceptionable soever ono ther
' accounts) ought to be rejected, *because* recom-
' mended by the *Provost*.'

The Scholars of the House are *sworn*, ' to obey
' the Provost in all things lawful and honest;'
they are consequently sworn, ' *Not to obey* the Pro-
' vost in any thing *Un*-lawful or *Dis*-honest:' the particularizing the qualifying circumstances sets limits to the duty, beyond which limits All is exception; and consequently the circumstances, contrary to those prescribed, must be forbidden; because two contraries cannot both be true. It is as unlawful and dishonest in a scholar, to be influenced

in

in his vote, as in a provoſt to influence : a ſcholar then, being ſworn, not to obey the provoſt in things unlawful and diſhoneſt, is conſequently ſworn, not to vote for any man whom the provoſt recommends.

But there needed not an oath to render it criminal and ſcandalous : all electors are bound by every tie of nature, law, and religion, to chooſe their parliamentary repreſentatives, according to the beſt of their *own* judgment, and not by the will of an *other* : it is a duty they owe, to God, that gives them a right to chooſe them ; to their country, that calls on them to exerciſe that right for the common good ; and to themſelves, in vindication of the honour it does them, and the liberty it ſecures to them. If any thing can aggravate guilt in one, more than in another, it muſt be his having a fuller knowledge of his duty, and a finer ſenſe of its obligations : if therefore it be ſcandalous and criminal in any elector, to be influenced, and conſequently corrupt ; it is certainly much more ſo, in a gentleman and a ſcholar.

It may be aſked, for I find you have put the queſtion, ſir, even in the public hall : ' ſhould ' the ſcholars reject a candidate of diſtinguiſhed ' worth and ability, merely for being recommend- ' ed by the provoſt ?' The queſtion is enſnaring to youth ; and was inſidiouſly propoſed, though no part of the lecture it was your buſineſs then to mind : it is a queſtion, which ſhews, there needs
no

no ghoſt to tell us, *who* put it into your mouth: but it is a queſtion, much eaſier to be anſwered, than fit to be propoſed; eſpecially by you, and in that publick place, and when it was your duty to talk of other matters. The anſwer is, *they ſhould.* They ſhould reject every man, for whom the proνoſt degrades himſelf to the abominable ſtate of a corruptor.

We are not do evil, for the attainment of good: nothing can be good, for which evil is committed, and if it could, the end cannot ſanctify the means, but the guilt of the means muſt pollute the end. The good we ſeek at an election, is very uncertain: the perſon we expect it from, may want the power, or the will, to effect it. The candidate, that thruſts himſelf forward, gives reaſon to ſuſpect his deſigns; the candidate that ſolicits votes by his friends, confeſſes a deficiency of merit in himſelf; and he, that has recourſe to the influence of authority or power, declares himſelf leagued againſt public liberty, by ſuch an attack on the freedom of election: a candidate therefore, that builds his ſucceſs on ſuch a foundation, betrays his want of thoſe qualifications, which alone ought to recommend him to the electors; and ſhews, it is not *their* intereſt he has at heart, but either *his own*, or that he is ſupported by.

Whether, therefore, we conſider the ſcholars of the houſe, as truſtees for the College, as young men

of

of virtue and sense, as in a state of probation for their future estimation, as assertors of the honour of their own families, or as examples to the other electors of the kingdom; I must still insist, " They ought not to vote for any man the provost recommends." Bad, as matters are in the world, men of worth are not so scarce, that as good may not be found, as any a provost can recommend; clear too, of that material disqualification: in regard therefore to their honour and their oath, for the honour of the college and their friends, for the sake of example, and for the publick good, SCHOLARS OF THE HOUSE *ought not to vote, for any man the* PROVOST *recommends.*

Such are the sentiments, sir, of every spirited and judicious

FATHER.

No. 10.   *Saturday, December* 17, 1774.

THE PUPIL's FIRST LETTER TO THE SCHOLARS
OF THE HOUSE.

Dear Lads,

ZEAL for the honour of the college has hurried us, I fear, into some inadvertency; and may make us liable, not only to deceive ourselves, but to be imposed on by others. Prejudice is prone, both to mistake and misrepresent; else we should not have seen such a letter, as lately appeared, against our worthy dean. Had the author known the dean, as my tutor does, he would not have judged so severely, or spoken so hardly, of his publick conduct. Little as ye think it, the dean is a very humane charitable man; and does more good, especially in the college, than he chooses himself to speak of: my tutor told me so; and I cannot doubt his word: his tutor told him so; and has too much gratitude, not to credit his patron's good report, especially from his own mouth. By whom

will

will a young man be influenced, if not by his tutor?

For these reasons, I not only excuse but commend my tutor, for embracing the opportunity of lecture hours to vindicate the doctor; and I hope, for the same reasons, I need not apologize for addressing you on the same subject. My tutor has exhorted and entreated all his pupils, to remove the impressions, which that letter else may leave upon your minds: and sure it is right in him, to justify the character he looks up to, as a model for his own; and to oblige a gentleman, he is so much obliged to himself. Is it not to him he owes his fellowship? and is it not to him he owes the exertion of all his powers? You will acknowledge, he could not employ the lecture hours much better; not more, at least, to his own satisfaction and our entertainment.

The dean's publick conduct indeed is generally deemed contemptible; but it has not been viewed in its proper light: he is accused of adulation to bishops and other men in power; but who can testify that? My tutor assures us, it is a malicious calumny; and indeed I never saw any thing like adulation about him: but I have never been in such company with the dean. His favour to the bishop's sons is no proof: for aught we know they may deserve it: and, if not they, perhaps his grace.
Which

Which of you would not be civil to the young gentlemen for a good living?

By other men in power, I suppose, the provost is glanced at; for he is a man in power, indeed. Has he not gotten a great pension, and amassed a great fortune too? Is he not a privy counsellor, and even prime to the prime serjeant? And is he not provost besides, though a layman and married; tho' utterly unacquainted with the constitution of the college, and unqualified even to sit for a junior fellowship? Has he not brought his son from abroad, to make him a member for the college? And has he not made him already, knight of the post; and sent him forth into the world to fight his battles, as the champion of domestick honour and paternal fame? *

Who, but the provost, dare openly employ bravoes, to blow a man's brains out, for telling him what he knew before? Who, but the provost, dare give publick notice, that vengeance is HIS; and that he has commissioned his son to execute it? Who, but the provost, dare paste up such a notice, not only in the college and the city, but even in the courts of justice, and even in the very presence of those sages, who are entrusted with the conservation of the laws?

He that can do such things, is undoubtedly a man in power; nay, may be considered, even as

men

* See No. 15.

men in power; for, can he not do what he will with all the men in power; and which of them can expect to prevail in any thing he disapproves of? Does he not exercise the power of provost in town, where he has no authority; and in a manner, the chief magistrate dares not attempt? And does he not neglect the duty of provost within the very walls of the college, when its statutes interfere with his attachments? Did he not overlook an illegal ridiculous challenge, fixed up in the college by one of its students; and soon after publickly censure the scholars of the house, for putting up a peaceable constitutioanl invitation?

The dean is his prime minister in the college: the dean knows the provost has been well paid for all his services; and may reasonably expect, to be well rewarded by him for his good offices.

PHIL. DIDACTOR.

No 11.

No. 11.   *Tuesday, December* 19, 1774.

THE PUPIL'S SECOND LETTER TO THE SCHO-
LARS OF THE HOUSE.

Dear Lads,

THE imputation the dean is branded with of opposing one provost, and violently prompting and supporting another, my tutor has declared to be as false as the other charges against him. Such of you, as were in the college then, ought now to stand forth; and make it appear, whether the letter-writer or my tutor tells the truth; and, until some such evidence clears the matter up, you cannot blame me, for taking my tutor's word; especially as the doctor's present conduct bears testimony to the assertion. But, allowing him as spirited in opposition to the late provost, as he is impetuous in favour of the present; you should consider, the cases are very different: the former indeed was *thought* a man of power, but the latter *is* so. What places or pensions did the other get, for all his bustle and jocularity? He made his uncle a bishop indeed; but it was by mere blustering and bullying: *this* has made himself provost; and,
notwithstanding

notwithstanding the many seeming improprieties of the appointment, was neither refused nor trifled with, like the other: some friends of the former (too) have been well provided for, but it was by College *Leases*, which the latter considers as not perfectly valid.

We are not to wonder then, if the doctor's conduct now appears a little different. Doctor *Andrews* neither wanted courage or good nature; neither was he so peevish or implacable: the present Dean therefore ran no great risk, in spiriting up the opposition against him, whether that provost were a good or a bad man. 'As a bad man, it was right to oppose him; and as a good man, it was not dangerous.' Skilful musicians adapt their airs to the nature of their instruments; neither should the Dean be condemned, for changing his tune now: for, if 'the provost be a good man, it is wrong to oppose him; and if a bad man, it is certainly dangerous.'

Ye will excuse my repeating his own words; for, my tutor confesses, the Dean *did* make use of this latter *Dilemma*. But he urged it, only from his regard for you; and to prevent the evils, which (he knew) you might expect, if you had persisted contumaciously disobedient. Besides he did not think you would have been so displeased: for, if his design was good, his argument was bad; and he knew, the retort of the Dilemma could not escape

escape you. Nay, he chose that form of persuasion on purpose: because, 'if he prevailed on you, you would have reason to thank him; and, if you perceived the weakness of his argument, you should be obliged to him' for not offering more cogent reasons, when he was sent to dissuade you from your favourite purpose.

The provost, it is true, under the disguise of *Moderator*, has allowed; that 'scholars of the house are entitled to all the rights of free electors; and that exercising such rights is neither inconsistent with good discipline, nor injurious to study: but, begging his Rt. Hon. pardon, I must agree with my tutor, that 'opposition to the provost is against the statutes.' No man understands the constitution, laws, and interest of the college, better than the dean: his new schemes and new regulations prove it; and, if it were not so, a gentleman so *learned*, *disinterested*, and *prudent* as the provost, would not be so guided and managed by him; consulting him on all his great concerns, as the princes of old did their sacred oracles.

Rebellion against government is treason by the law; your opposition to the provost, therefore, is unlawful. The statutes expressly forbid conspiracies against him; associations therefore, in support of constitutional rights, are contrary to the statutes, and to *obey* the provost in all things lawful and honest; nothing can be honest, that leads to the violation

lation of an oath, or that is contrary to law; your confultations for the maintenance of independence therefore, being difpleafing to the provoft, are unlawful and difhoneft. If you fay, that what I render by the word honeft, may be more properly interpreted decent or honourable, confider, how indecent and difhonourable it is, to violate an oath; and be convinced from the provoft's promotion, that ' no man *now* can become *right* honourable, by holding fuch publick meetings, and fhewing fuch publick fpirit as you do.'

How much more prudent was my tutor's conduct at the laft election! he fays, *he voted on both fides:* and you may be fure, he fought under his tutor's aufpices. Imitate, dear lads, his guarded conduct; and fo defend yourfelves with a two-edged fword, as the dean does now with his *dilemma*.

PHIL. DIDACTOR.

No. 12.

No. 12.   *Saturday, December 24, 1774.*

THE PUPIL'S THIRD LETTER TO THE SCHOLARS OF THE HOUSE.

Dear Lads,

WHAT has bewitched you? Are you callous to the touches of humanity? Are you deaf to the calls of pity? You have ruined my *tutor*; you have set the dean mad; and I fear you will break the poor *provost's* heart. If you persevere in your taunts, and gibes, and satyrick pleasantries; or carry your opposition and resentment any farther; you will certainly have three lives to answer for.

After all I had said, in vindication of my tutor, and in justification of the doctor, I hoped, you would be sensible of your extravagance, and amend: but the more you are cautioned, reproached, and threatened, the more obstinate and perverse you grow. When the provost himself reasoned with you in the character of *Moderator*, you called his assertions lies, his arguments quibbles, his meekness hypocrisy, and his exhortations cant:

again,

again, when my tutor (under the signature of *Eusebius*) reminded you of the doctor's inflexible consistency, and temperate zeal, and sedate *humility*, and sweet good humour; you ridiculed his pathetick descriptions as fustian rant, and the instance of the doctor's charity as a silly tale. Nay, to aggravate your *atrocious* crimes, you add insult to rebellion; and, to the provost's face, mock his concern for discipline, and the attachment of his friends.

What is it you would be at? Do you pretend to more wisdom and virtue, than your betters; and set up for reformers, in such times as these? Can you suppose yourselves fitter judges of parliamentary merit, than the provost; or able to hold out against that persuasion, which has convinced so many great lords, and famed orators, and flaming patriots, of the folly of stubborn opposition now? Shall boys baffle that sophistry, which has prevailed on squires, to load the inheritance of their children; on peers, to ennoble bastardy; on plunderers, to share the spoil; and on instruments of despotism, to make a *little blustering coxcomb* independent? Take my word for it; if you make any more stir about freedom of election, not a man of you need expect a fellowship, during the *incumbance* of the present provost: my tutor says, the doctor is sure of it; and therefore since he cannot influence you by his lectures, he has declared he will write to your friends.

The

The provost is resolved, the *college* shall be like other boroughs: it was a stipulated condition: and would you have a senator, a privy-counsellor, and a provost break his word? Promises are sacred engagements; and the secret articles of treaties are always the most religiously observed.

In justice therefore, lay aside your resentment at the *provost*; he only studies to promote your interest: in gratitude, put an end to your sarcasms on the *dean* and my *tutor*; they only wish, to preserve you from harm. Can you suspect such worthy, steady, sweet, good men, capable of being the dupes of ambition and avarice? Can you impute to such base purposes, my *tutor*'s POLITICAL LECTURES, or the *doctor*'s DILEMMA.

PHIL. DIDACTOR.

No. 13.   *Monday, December 26, 1774.*

Confiteor si quid prodest delicta fateri.   OVID.

TO THE PRINTER OF THE HIBERNIAN
JOURNAL.

SIR,

IN the course of last week I was summoned frequently to attend boards at the provost-house, in order to answer for my *unpardonable* offence in
reading

reading news-papers. One day, in the passage to his hall, I found the following letter, addressed to you; and as it manifestly was Doctor F—r—s—th's intention to have it published, I imagine I shall do but common justice to his much-wounded character, by transmitting it to you.

I am, Sir,

Your constant Reader,

A Scholar of the House.

TO THE PRINTER OF THE HIBERNIAN JOURNAL.

SIR,

As many false, scandalous and scurrilous papers, filled with gross lies, and reflecting on my character, have been lately published, and as no body has endeavoured to answer all the charges urged against me; I am compelled to undertake, myself, a vindication of my conduct, and a general defence of the propriety of my behaviour. No body that knows me ever suspected that I gave a dinner to any bishop through friendship; it is notorious, from my former violent declarations against them, that I would not submit to their acquaintance, if I was not convinced it would have served either my own interest, or my friend's. What fools the fellows are to think that that could be done by any means but adulation?

adulation? ay, ay, my character will be hurt, to be sure, by its being said, " I was great with Bishops." I was accused, too, with having disapproved of the scholar's assembly: It is a well-known fact, that I *made* every body I was *sure* would vote for the provost, go to the meeting to support his interest. What! though I scolded all the independents, as they called themselves, for provoking so *worthy* a man by their conduct, is that a reason for charging me with censuring, indiscriminately, every man that met? The dilemma I do not dispute, as I think it an excellent argument; but I will clearly refute the assertion of my guiding the provost; for so far is it from being true, that it is notorious he absolutely guides *me*, and that I never have disputed any of his commands; and why should I? Has not he given me offices to the amount of two hundred and thirty-one pounds per ann. which is three times more than any other junior fellow ever had before? Were not some even left without places, in order that I might be *sufficiently* provided for? Would you have me be guilty of the basest ingratitude? and now I mention ingratitude, it puts me in mind of a damned villain's assertion, that I charged some scholars with it, for not avowing the same principles with myself: It is false; it is false. I only said it was cruel and scandalous of them, when I had made promises for them all to the provost, to make a liar of me by behaving like *gentlemen*, forsooth. How can I shew my face to the man, after their infamous baseness in refusing me
their

their votes? to shew them the folly of their proceedings, I made use of invincible reasoning; but, would you think it? I could not convince the puppies That the publick may see that they were guided intirely by a spirit of faction, I will mention one of my strongest arguments.——If a difficulty, said I, occurred to you in any of your sciences, to whom would you apply? to me, certainly, or some other fellow; why, then, in any affair of so much consequence, should such rash, giddy boys as you, be suffered to make use of their own reason? It is evident you should let your tutors judge for you. The truth of this position is so manifest, that I will say no more on that head. I never wrote to any man's father since I left off taking pupils; If H—s wrote to them by my directions, ought I to be charged with it in a public paper? it was said, also, that he, poor little fellow, exposed himself in vindicating me, and the provost. It is a damned lie; he defended us very well, and very humourously; for every body, I am told, that heard him, could not help laughing. I was charged with inconsistency in opposing the late provost, and supporting the present What did I ever get from Andrews, that I should support him? did he ever make an extraordinary distinction between me and the other fellows, though H—s had as many pupils, scholars of the house, before his death as he has at present? did I not receive from the present provost a *substantial* mark of esteem on the disposal of offices? and am not I promised, whenever an opportunity offers,

that

that his whole interest shall be exerted in my favour? as I do not know the persons who wrote to me, I inform them, whoever they are, through your paper, that I despise them as much as they despise me. I am sure they are scholars of the college; but I am not at all vexed; I would not give the fellows the satisfaction of putting myself in a passion; but if I can find them out——

I have unluckily made a rash vow, that I never would subscribe my own name to any letter in the publick papers; I am therefore obliged to make use of the nick-name, by which I am distinguished in the college. I am convinced, from your known impartiality, that as the charges against me have been published, you will also publish my defence.

I am, Sir,

Your very humble servant,

NATHAN BEN SADDI.

No. 14.   *Tuesday, December 27, 1774.*

Hic niger est—hunc tu Romane caveto.   Hor.
Non tu, Pomponi, cæna diserta tua est.   Mart.

TO THE REV. THOMAS TORRENS, J. F. TRINITY COLLEGE.

SIR,

FROM the respect due to a fellow of our college, but more especially on account of that secret esteem had to yourself, I am induced to address you, on an event which seems to engage all our attention.

For many years past has the name of Torrens sounded with unusual delight, in the ear of every student; and well it might, as no man ever kept in that happy line, which distinguishes too great severity from an over-easiness better than you did, whether I consider you in the capacity of dean, or tutor. In the round of toasts, where none but men of worth were drank, you always led the van. Mr. Waller was called the honest, but you the *very* honest fellow. This, Sir, was formerly the case; but, alas! how changed!—And why all this?

this! Becaufe you have undertaken to fupport Black Phill*, as a candidate for our univerfity; a wretch fo deteftable,—fo odious to every one of us, that a fiend from the Tartarian regions would be as grateful to every elector.

But he fets up, I am told, for independence: heaven and earth be witnefs, if this be tolerable! Shall that man, who, on every occafion fuppreffed truth, and trampled on liberty, become now an advocate for independency? Surely thofe gentlemen, who all, to *a man*, I truft, have hearts impregnated with generous principles, will treat fuch confummate audacioufnefs as it deferves. For my part,

---

* The Right Hon. P——p T——l, his majefty's attorney general, fecretary of ftate, and judge of the prerogative court. Of this gentleman the following character is given by a contemporary hiftorian:——" He was a man formed by nature, and fafhioned by long practice for all manner of court intrigue. His ftature was low, fo as to excite neither envy nor obfervation; his countenance difmal; his public manners grave; and his addrefs humble. But as in publick he covered his *proftitution* by a folemnity of carriage, fo in private he endeavoured to captivate by convivial humour, and to difcountenance *all publick virtue*, by the exercife of a perpetual, and fometimes not unfuccefsful irony.——To thefe qualifications he added an extraordinary magnificence of living. His table was furnifhed with every thing that fplendour could fuggeft, or luxury could confume; and his profufion and *policy* united to folicit a multitude of guefts. To his houfe then reforted all thofe who wifhed through him to obtain, or learn from him to enjoy without remorfe, thofe publick emoluments, which are the purchafe of *publick infidelity*."

part, as an elector, I will; and join with those my worthy and spirited brother scholars (whose names I would gladly set forth in golden letters, were I not certain the world would soon know them) in every proper scheme, to manifest our resentment, and *reject* the man. Let us then, my friends, stick close to each other, and spurn those private inuendoes, thrown out every day. By these means we will obtain our end, and set an example for the present constituents, throughout the whole kingdom, as well as future ages. If we fail, this pleasing idea will still remain, that we acted rightly; but if victory crowns our endeavours, how superlatively glorious will be our success.

And now, Sir, I entreat, I conjure you not to persevere in supporting *such a man*, at the expence of our warm esteem. Every attachment must now be laid aside, which acts repugnant to our country's interest. *Cari sunt patres, Cari sunt liberi, Cari sunt amici, sed omnes caritates complectitur patria.* We will suspend our opinion for some time; if nothing is done mean while, you may expect to hear from me soon.

A Scholar of the House.

No. 15.

No. 15.   *Thursday, December* 29, 1774.

Crudum manduces Priamum Priamique pisinnos?
Troy and her people wouldst thou eat alive,
And eat up Priam and his children all?   HOBBES.

AN HEROIC EPISTLE FROM BIDDY FITZPATRICK, Nursery-maid to the right honourable John Hely Hutchinson, provost of Trinity College, Dublin, to William Doyle, Esq; as it was rejected by the *impartial* committee of the *Free-Press.*

ADVERTISEMENT.

I SHOULD not have thrown aside the native reserve of my sex, by appearing thus in publick, had not the respectable society, of which I have the honour to be a member, been so boldly defy'd, by the gentleman, to whom the following lines are addressed.——He has thrown down the glove, in these words: —" I republish the letter, which you are pleased to approve. " Its expressions are as irretractable, as its principles.—I must " repeat every passage, even though I should make a *nursery* my " enemies."‡ I *hereby* give the gentleman fair warning—let him pursue hostilities at his peril.—   BIDDY FITZPATRICK.

AS beauteous Helen (bane and boast of Troy)†,
In shining armour, deck'd the Trojan Boy,
Rous'd him, from revel, minstrelsy, and dance,
To wield the buckler, and to hurl the lance;

From

‡ See the answer of William Doyle, Esq; to an address presented to him by Mr. James Napper Tandy,—published in the Freeman's Journal.

† We need not be surpris'd at this young lady's erudition—it was but natural that the president of a learned seminary should require an attention to literature, even in his nursery maid.

From soft embraces, and the bed of down,
In laurell'd fields to purchase fair renown;
Resign'd her pleasure, for the hero's fame;
And cry'd " go forth and earn a deathless name."

   Divine *Salvagni* sends her hero forth,
To prove, in Freeman's Journal, patriot worth.
From melting airs, and soft Italian sounds,
From luring eyes with sly insidious wounds,
From am'rous parley, from delightful war,
And gentle fights—yet not without a scar,
She sends him forth to wield the grey-goose pen,
And scourge the publick deeds of publick men;
With *gentle lisp*, she cries,—to arms!—to arms!
And *alma mater* hears the wild alarms.

   Where, (mighty spirit!) hast thou lain conceal'd?
At most, seen dimly—in thy works reveal'd—
Hast thou with wild prophetic fury fir'd,
To deep retreats, and sacred shades retir'd?
Thou new Tiresias! to foresee the doom
Of future patriots, candidates to come;
What future honour, or what future fight
With May'r or Shrieve awaits Belcampo's knight;
With free-born hand, what legal pioneer
Shall rase the walls, and turrets of Blaquiere;
What sunday-prentice through the park shall scour,
And proudly break his neck to show his pow'r;
What toils, what cares, what murmurs has it cost!
On Liffey's bank to seek her patriot lost?—
                                    Where

Where with his trident sea-born Achmet rules,
O'er jets, and fountains, bagnios, pumps and pools;
Tremendous Beckford,— hell-born Donoghoe,
And scowling bailiffs,—(a nefarious crew)
Unwelcome visitants—impetuous rove;
The bagnio ransack; and o'erturn the stove;
The closets rummage; in the cauldron pry;
And not a couch escapes their impious eye.———
While various tasks the triton race engage,
For every sex design'd,—and every age:
Some—wither'd maids in vats of pickle lave;
And each—a venus, rises from the wave:
Some—potent drugs and herbs in cauldrons brew,
That modern Esons into youth renew:
Some boil to mucilage, the tender beau;
And blushes some, on palefac'd maids bestow.
From baths and cauldrons, frighted patients fly,
And shrieks and curses rend the midnight sky.
In blankets some (like bedlamites) conceal'd,
And some (scant covering) scarce by napkin veil'd,
Dislodg'd from covert like the frighted hare,
With locks dishevell'd, and with members bare,
Shudd'ring with cold and wild affright they scud;
And shrink, before the legal sons of blood.

Why now at last with sword and lance appear,
To fill a *nursery*, with pallid fear?
To whip the children, kick the nurs'ry maid,
And make the very cat and dog afraid.
Monster! more fell than nursing legend knows,
Avaunt! avaunt! nor murder our repose.

Ah

Ah wilt thou dash the babes against the stones?
And suck their blood and cranch their little bones?
Why on the nurselings must thy fury fall?
What, all my little ones?—thou tyrant!—all?
No warlike din affrights this peaceful throng;
But all is slumber, lullaby and song.
No horror turns the cheek to ashy pale,
Save when the nurse recounts her wizzard tale.
No *rawhead* terrifies the gentle train,
No *bloodybones* deforms the smiling scene.

But say—what vengeance shall th' invader feel,
Who threats a *nursery* with savage steel?

Our eldest hope, our young *Iulus* stands,
Th' avenging pistols glitter in his hands;
Forth from this * *great society* he flies;
(Though nurse recalls and little brother cries)
Rous'd like a lion from his wicker cage,
Indignant marks thy *blind* impetuous rage;
With stealthy peace thy dark retreat pervades;
And finds the Cacus, in his circling shades.—

I too—will hurl my saucepan at thy head;
Milk and panada, shall thy face o'erspread.

Far-

---

* " Regard to my own character, as a gentleman, and re-
" spect for the *great society*, to which *I belong*, make me ab-
" stain from using any opprobrious terms."—Vide, a letter to
William Doyle, Esq; republished in the Freeman of November the 19th.

Far other gift the chambermaid shall pour,
And drench thy visage, in far other show'r.
A blanket—yes—a blanket fates decree—
A lofty blanketing, thy meed shall be.
Four brawny chairmen shall the corners grace,
Four buxom wenches, shall the patriot place
On woven billow, that with active spring,
Its restless burthen to the roof shall fling.
There, like some pan-cake turn'd,—and toss'd on high,
There shall the hero tumble, flounce and fry.
Then shalt thou dream, of being chair'd in state;
On weavers' necks up-borne (a welcome weight).
What shall it boot how bright thy courage glow'd?
Or what the civick box on Wilkes bestow'd?
Ah what the wreath imputed essays yield?
Or what the myrtle earn'd in Paphian field?
Not Newenham shall save thee from our hate,
Not Napper Tandy shall avert thy fate.
No, should thy Lucas (awful shadow) rise,
Shake goes the blanket, and the patriot flies :
Flies like a *shuttlecock* through airy plains,
While mounting feather solid log sustains.
Around *free citizens* (a sapient band)
And *Skinner's-alley aldermen* shall stand:
The mighty Sheridan with aching sight,
Shall trace the patriot in his airy flight.
At length some god shall snatch him from afar,
And fix him in the heav'ns, a blazing star:
A blazing star, in *alma mater*'s tail;
To Provosts, boding fate and ruin pale.

Th'

Th' attempt, such dangers, and such glory wait.—
Come 'prove the good and evil, of thy fate!

BIDDY FITZPATRICK.

No 16.   *Friday, December 30, 1774.*

Ἵππαρχοι κρεμασας μαστιγωσον.
           PLUT. in ANT. ED. BRY. V. 140.

TO HIPPARCHUS.

A MAN whose conduct, O! *Hipparchus!* claims universal hatred, may wonder at finding one who pities him!——but your ambition and vanity combine with your present embarrassment to produce a situation which *malice* itself might compassionate. Your dreams of projected tyranny fade, to your mortification, as an ambitious—your abilities, doubtful before, are now ascertained to your confusion, as a vain man. I pity you—or rather the state which suffers in you;—for when the head becomes ridiculous, the body must endure its share of contempt.

Bustling, forward, assuming, and loquacious, you rose to honours;—not by superior genius—your pleadings, your oratory in the senate, prove the
contrary

contrary ;—not by professional knowledge—there you are notoriously shallow and impotent ;—not by the talents of business—let your conduct in your new station speak for itself ;—but by your *vanity*, as infinite in its pretences, as impudent in maintaining them. The firmness of your voice, your boldness in pronouncing, and unblushing defence of error, bullied men into an half acknowledgment of your abilities ; and while you seemed so perfectly assured of your own merit, the world grew weary or ashamed of disputing the claim. Men are generally unkind to demands for fame and honour ;—their courtesy to your's was signal and lavish ;—it was your own task to prove it injudicious.

When you solicited an employment, for which, by your profession, principles, and studies, you seemed eminently disqualified, the malicious waited, in impatient suspense, for the ominous excursions of a planet that had so wildly rushed from its usual system ;—they were astonished, not disappointed : but the candid, who seeing you in an employment so different from any you had formerly filled, hoped that you had changed your character, and *expected some good from you.*

Yet even here you justified the opinion entertained by some, of your being an extraordinary man : The poor ostentation of address, the meagre parade of abilities and learning, might have escaped with contempt (the emotion proper to them) it required

your

your uncommon talents to make them objects of hatred.

You soon commenced tyrant, and our tyranny has been a defultory, unmeaning, wanton oppreſſion; more like the wayward petulance of a *ſickly child*, or the teaſing uſurpation of a weak woman, than the calm, confiſtent, ſteady meaſures of a reaſonable man; an oppreſſion tolerable only in this—that a thouſand laughable abſurdities in the man, the miniſtry, and mode of exertion, make the tyranny ridiculous, and afford the ſufferers a jeſt in their miſery.

You, like the angel in one of our poets, or rather, the theatrical dæmon in another, ſeem to delight to ride in the whirlwind;—but is it to your honour to *raiſe* a ſtorm which you are unable to *direct?*

There is a littleneſs, a meanneſs in anonymous publications, even in a good cauſe, which can only be excuſed by the want of another channel for communicating ſentiments which ought not to be concealed. The taſk may be uſeful; it never is honourable. It is a new thing to ſee the head of a great and learned ſociety rank with the humble band of newſpaper pioneers, that facilitate in ſecret the operations of party; to ſee the ſhepherd of a learned flock ſend his verboſe productions (in the form of paſtoral letters,) to propagate idle prolixity,

and

and despicable sophistry through the kingdom. †
At your accession, you proposed to encourage
composition in the society over which you preside;—did you mean to encourage it likewise in the
political writers of the town, by giving a subject in
your conduct, and an example in your compositions?

By this ridiculous sensibility, you confirmed the
opinion of your weakness, already excited by the
choice of your premier ‡.—A man, who happily
unites the peculiar vices of a convent and a court:
hot, persecuting, vindictive, prejudiced, and bigotted, without honesty; artful, plotting, intriguing, insincere, and unfriendly, without gentleness
or politeness. His injudicious precipitance has
caused more mischief, than his zeal and profligacy
can remedy.

Under the appearance of superior learning and
piety, this man has endeavoured to pervert the young
mind with scandalous sophistry and miserable casuistry, and dared to preach those base sentiments,
which (though many practise) only the rash bigotry
of a cloister would avow. His conduct, indeed,
confirms the observation, that of all vices, those of a
Saint are most odious, shameless, and unrelenting.
What pleasure would it give a *deist* to see the profession of piety rendered odious, by the practice of

a *very*

---

† See No. 3.
‡ Dr. F——h.

a *very religious man*; to find a spy and an informer in the priesthood.

We may trace the rashness of your prompter, in the attempt to introduce inquisition practices, and monkish trials; to establish within those walls, (where the course of study excites, and the form of government ought to cherish liberality of sentiment) a star-chamber,—to defend the dread majesty of great men, and great prerogative, by the multiplied terrors of informations, accusations, examinations, vexations, insults, reprimands and disapprobations. Your miniature of archbishop Laud, has invented for you new branches of prerogative, to be asserted; new crimes, new violations to be punished.

Armed with the doctrine of libels (that formidable engine of oppression in all tyrannies) you have invaded the student, even in his own province. You have opened a wide field for accusation, and made it necessary for him to fee a lawyer, before he opens a new volume. †

The subtilty of a veteran lawyer has been employed to ensnare the open artlessness of youth; to draw generous simplicity into self-crimination. Such are your arts of government; and their effect has

† Alluding to several students being cited and *threatned* to be censured by Hipparchus for the *high misdemesnor* of *reading* a newspaper; on which important occasion *nine* conclaves were held.

has been, difhonour to yourfelf———ftrength to oppofition. Your conduct has been fet in the moft contemptible light, by that of the electors, which has difplayed a calm intrepidity, a dignified decency of oppofition, which would do honour to mature manhood.

You are a vain weak man, in a ridiculous, perplexed fituation; and as fuch I advife you to retract in time. Your counfellor is an ambitious, rafh, timid, indifcreet man; ignorant of the temper, carelefs of the interefts of your fubjects. The reft of your adherents want honefty and courage to controvert meafures, which they muft condemn. They indulge a difeafed adminiftration, to its perdition; and the fruits of fuch counfels, muft be outrage, inconfiftency, abfurdity and fhame.

Since you cannot fubdue, ceafe to perfecute; fuperintend the erection of your riding houfe. Let it fatisfy your vaft ambition, to have gained the hatred of the prefent generation. Seek not the crimes of the future, by ruining the feat of education.

CHARIDEMUS.

No. 17.

No. 17.   *Monday, January 9, 1775.*

*Duplex Libelli dos eft : Quod Rifum movet,
Et quod Prudenti Vitam Confilio monet.*   PHÆD.

THE VOTE-TRAP:
OR,
A NEW ART OF ELECTIONEERING:
A
DIALOGUE.

SCENE.
Dr. Pompofo's Chambers in the College.

PRANCERO, POMPOSO.

Prancero.

WHAT a dreadful fituation, Pompofo, am I in? One of the great objects, you know, which I had in view, in my prefent eccentrick promotion, was to get the feals. With one foot on the college fteeple and the other on the fecretary's office, I thought I could eafily jump into the chancellor's feat. I muft own, my friend, Sir Spindle Barebones, has kept his word with me. He is now in London, and has done every thing in his power;—has *memorialed—reprefented—mifreprefented*—but I fear all
will

will not do. This patriot Englifh Irifh chancellor, with his curfed popularity, has marred our fcheme; and what is more provoking, the fellow feems to laugh at our impotent endeavours to undermine him. But let that pafs—my grand object of all, as I have told you, was to make the univerfity a fnug borough, to nominate two members; and with them and my nominee for Lanefborough at my heels, I fhould have fuch a *following*, that I fhould be able to obtain half a dozen more reverfions for myfelf and my children. To be foiled here——" *here where I had garnered up my heart*"——were fuch perdition, that the very thought of it makes me fhudder.

Pompofo. Thefe young men have ftrange notions, that's the truth of it; and they feem to be fo clofely linked together, to be animated with fuch a fpirit, and to be actuated with fo genuine a love of freedom and independency, that I fear it will be a very *operofe* tafk to work upon them. But, at all events, you know you can nominate about a dozen fcholars next Whitfontide; and although they, with about half of the fellows, and a few ftragglers from the adverfary's camp, will not make a majority, yet fo high an act of power will ferve to intimidate the reft, and by fhewing them that no college honours are to be obtained but by compliance with your requifitions, frighten thefe *peftilent* voters into your meafures, or render their *oppugnation futile* and inefficacious.

Prancero.

Prancers. It will be a daring attempt, and I fear were I to do it, the house of commons would set them aside as occasional voters; as they did in old Baldwin's time.—But no matter.—I am now so deeply engaged that I must stop at nothing.—But, my dear friend, that time is far off, and perhaps a dissolution of parliament may take place between this and then. May we not do something in the mean while? This *Dr. Dilemma* †, whom I have too rashly confided in, is so proud, so uncomplying, so passionate, and has withal so much of monkish severity about him, that, although he is ready enough to do the meanest offices for me, yet he has rather estranged and exasperated the boys than conciliated them to me: and, to own the truth, my own measures have, I fear, been too violent, and seem rather to have cemented than loosened the opposition. They begin to talk loudly of my breaking through the stated order of college appointments, and of my thrusting a creature of my own into an office to which he was not entitled, for the purpose of making him a *Spy* upon their actions—of my having erected an *Inquisition* within these walls, and endeavoured to restrain even the freedom of thought—of my arraigning students for imputed offences, undescribed by the statutes ‡—of my inveigling them to criminate themselves—and after a tedious and nugatory examination, dismissing them with a sort of Delphick Sentence, so very ambiguous
that

† Dr. F—s—tb.
‡ Several students were cited before the board for reading a newspaper in the College Hall.

that they could not appeal from it, becaufe forfooth no one could underftand it. This and a great deal more has been faid, and I muft own not without foundation. You remember, my dear doctor, one of them, † whom I haraffed for three days at the board (who, unfortunately for us, had fo amiable a character, and behaved with fuch moderation and decorum that we could not venture to meddle with him) had the impudence to afk me to give him a copy of my fentence in writing; no doubt, for the purpofe of appealing to the vifitors. The fellow wanted me to give the *unfubftantial nothing* a being and a name.—But I wander from my point.—What can we do with thefe refolute, impracticable fcholars?

Pompofo. Why, in God's name, fince violence has not fucceeded, you may effay the effect of more pacific operations.——Adulation, adulation, is the grand arcanum; as my poor friend Andrews ufed to fay.——You are, you know, foon to erect a theatre for the purpofe of teaching the rifing generation the arts of elocution, oratory, and *fuch like:* thofe arts, of which you are at once fo admirable a model and fo exquifite a judge. Now, fuppofe I were, under the guife of a preparatory courfe, to collect as many of the fcholars of the houfe as I can, two or three times a week (taking care always to mingle fome non-electors along with them as a cloak to our defign) and initiate them in the arts of pronunciation, enunciation,

† Mr. *Palmer.*

enunciation, and *such like*, by assigning them certain portions of Shakespeare, Milton, &c. to recite. I will *delate* to you those scholars who are the most active agitators for freedom and independence, whom it is most important for you to court *urgently*, and who will most *difficultly* be wrought upon. Then you may *purposedly* drop in, as it were by accident, and by high encomiums on their performance worm yourself — you understand me —

Prancero. Perfectly. — Ten thousand thanks, my dear Pomp. " Thou art the best of cut-throats." — I beseech you lose no time, but run immediately and bring in as many of the scholars as you can meet with ——— I'll retire into the next room; and presently when you are all in the middle of the pandemonium or the Capitol, drop in among you.

Pomposo. I fly to execute your mandates; nor shall I ever *succumb* under any task you are pleased to impose upon me.

[Pomposo *goes out, and* Prancero *retires into an adjoining chamber.* ——— *After a short absence* Pomposo *returns with half a dozen scholars*]

Pomposo. Be so good, Sir Classick, and Sir Silverton, to open the celebrated scene in Julius Cæsar, between Brutus and Cassius.

[*Scholars read.*]

Pomposo.

Pomposo. Bene — Euge — admirable indeed ! — But whom do I see ? — I protest our amiable P—— has condescended——

Prancero (entering). Gentlemen, I beg you'll keep your seats—Sir Classick—Sir Silverton—pray go on ;—I shall be glad to take a lesson from two young gentlemen of whose excellent elocution I have heared so much, since my promotion to the high office I have now the honour to enjoy.

Sir *Silverton.*
You have done that you should be sorry for ;
There is no terror, Cassius, in your threats,
For I am arm'd so strong in honesty,
That they pass by me as the idle wind
That I respect not ; I did send to you
For certain sums of gold, which you deny'd me,
For I can raise no money by vile means ;
By heav'n, I had rather coin my heart,
And drop my blood for drachma's, than to wring
From the hard hands of peasants their vile trash
By any indirection : I did send
To you for gold to pay my legions,
Which you deny'd me ; was that done like Cassius ?
Shou'd I have answer'd Caius Cassius so ?
When Marcus Brutus grows so covetous,
To lock such rascal counters from his friends ;
Be ready gods with all your thunder bolts,
Dash him to pieces.

Prancero.

Prancero. (Aside) [not raise money by vile means! What an ideot! but as Oliver Cromwell used to say, I must talk to these fellows in their own way]——Excellent Brutus! how noble, how generous, how disinterested!—Sir Classick pray proceed.

(Sir Classick and Sir Silverton finish the scene.)

Prancero. Fine enunciation!——So free from any provincial accent——so void of any false tones!——I shall be happy, Dr. Pomposo, to shew these young gentlemen, who are such proficients in the most difficult of all the arts, every favour in my power.——*I care not whether they vote for me or against me,*——Merit shall be rewarded.——But, gentlemen, at our next meeting, I hope you will bring Thucydides and Demosthenes with you. At Eton, my son tells me, they can construe either of them at sight. The oration of *Pericles* will be a fine piece for you to pronounce. In the mean while, to come nearer home, permit me to give you some instructions with respect to speaking in parliament; that great theatre of modern elocution. Such of you as are designed for the pulpit I leave to Dr. Pomposo, than whom no man is master of a more sonorous, nervous and persuasive eloquence. But for parliamentary haranguing I will yield to no man. The first thing you must attend to is your dress; no man was ever listened to who was not well dressed; and when your years require you to wear a wig, you must take care to have at least 300 rows of curls

in

in it. The next thing,——but I have not time to discuss this matter thoroughly. There are however two or three short rules which you must never forget;——begin always with telling your audience, that the subject of their consideration is the most *important* that ever was agitated in that assembly; (no matter what the question may be; the erection of a coal-yard; widening Corke harbour, or any thing else) Then be sure to repeat again, and again, that you will make your positions as clear as the *Day-light*. If any objection has been made by your opponents, which stands plump in the way of these *Day-light Propositions*, if you have no answer ready, which probably will be the case, you may say, you will come to *that* by-and by,---and take care *never* to come to it. Ay but say you, this will never do without a little argument;---why, as for that you may always contrive to speak pretty late in the debate;-- Glean up all the best arguments that have been used by those who have gone before you on the same side of the question;---clothe them in pretty smooth language;---Be sure round all your periods well;---If sorely pushed, call your adversaries factious blockheads---Artificers of attitudes—spouters of periods---dealers in seven-syllabled phraseology,---barbers boys,---bungling incendiaries,-- or any other names that come into your head;---and when nothing else will go down, stop their mouths with some stale precedent, or obsolete act of parliament; (no matter whether there be such a one or not) if you are challenged to point out the place, take up

the

the statute book, and affect great surprise at not being able to find it, although perhaps you ransacked the book in vain for it, the whole day before—*Probatum est.*—But I fear I am tiresome. Pray, Sir Classick, will you be so good as to open Waller or Prior;—the Doctor, I dare say, has them;—you are fond, I am told of the lighter poetry—or perhaps you will favour us with some collegiate production.——I hope soon to institute premiums for the *Improvement of Composition*.—And though I can't help lamenting, that by the most unwarrantable and premature practices, a flame has been kindled within these walls, which by the greatest *moderation* and propriety of conduct, I have endeavoured to allay, yet at the same time it gives me infinite satisfaction to observe that the late contests have drawn forth bashful merit from its retreat. The poem which was published in the name of my son's nurse, is indeed a master-piece, and would have done honour to Pope.

Sir Classick. With your permission then, Sir, I will read you a little *Jeu d'esprit*, which has just appeared. (*Reads,*)

On the GENTLEMEN of the UNIVERSITY being permitted to *dance* during THE SATURNALIA.

Hark, what glad sound, the darkling cloister chears!
A dance, a dance—the festal band appears :
                                            A dance,

A dance, a dance, the vaulted halls refound;
A dance, a dance, the *Freshmen* shout around.
A fidler—hark! he strikes the trembling string,
According foot-steps through the cloisters ring;
Now shall the gouty man his crutch forego,
And leap exulting like the powder'd beau:
Each college duty shall be done in dance,
And hopeful students shall not walk but—*prance*.

Prancero. What a bitter dog! he has difcharged one of the enemy's pieces full in my bofom;—but I muft admire it. [*Afide*.
He-he, very pleafant indeed;—he-he, the true Attick Salt!

Pompofo, (waking.) Blefs me! where am I? What can be the matter?—The little gentleman is quite pale;—he looks at once *diftreffed* and *lively*, and will, I am fure, be glad to get away. [*Afide*.] Excellent Sir, I admire how, in the multiplicity of your avocations, you have been able not only to fathom the profundities of ancient literature, but to acquire, at the fame time, a tafte for the more exquifite graces of lighter compofitions. But, indeed, this is too much—after all the labours of the day— the board—the bar—the council—(to fay nothing of your private lucubrations)—you muft be enormoufly fatigued; if you pleafe, therefore, we will break off for the prefent; and I hope thefe gentlemen who have made fo *aufpicious* a beginning, will foon favour me with their company again.

Prancero.

Prancero. Well, since you will have it so, we'll have done for the present, though I am charmed with this morning's entertainment;—but I hope to have many such—and shall always be happy to shew every scholar, of whatever party, and *let him vote how he may*, every countenance in my power, and to instruct them, to the best of my poor abilities, in the great arts of pronunciation, enunciation, and elocution.

[*Exeunt omnes.*]

※※※※※※※※※※※※※※※※※※※※※※※※

No. 18.   *Wednesday, January 11, 1775.*

Dixit adhuc aliquid? nil sane.   Hor.

TO THE PUBLICK.

HOWEVER improper it may appear in the head of so learned a Seminary, and so respectable a Society as this, over which I have the honour to preside, to engage in a news-paper contention, and to enter into a publick discussion, and into a publick defence of that conduct, and those measures, which have been malignly attacked by anonymous adversaries; yet, inspired by my zeal for the welfare of the University (in which the welfare of the kingdom is materially involved), and with
a view

a view of removing the mists of prejudice and error, industriously spread before the intellectual eyes of inexperienced young men, in order to mislead their judgment, and to cause them to deviate from the secure paths of salutary discipline, into the dangerous walk of unjustifiable faction, I again appeal to the candour, sense and experience of my countrymen; and, permit me to add, I entertain the most sanguine hopes that this publick address will entirely extinguish those ferments which my first happily allayed.

I am confident that I will prove to demonstration, and make it as clear as the *day-light*, that the measures which I have pursued, since my appointment, have been dictated by wisdom, and are founded in virtue; I will remove every shadow of doubt from the minds of gentlemen who peruse my letters. But, first, let me observe, that the subject now laid before the publick is of the greatest *importance*; and, let me entreat my countrymen seriously to turn it in their thoughts, to afford it that dignified attention, that unprejudiced examination which its magnitude merits; a conduct eminently coincident with their national character, since it is universally acknowledged, that their patience, their fairness, their deliberative dignity, when matters of public import are referred to their consideration, can only be equalled by the justice and impartiality of their decisions. The present subject is, perhaps, the most material that ever engaged the public attention. The Provost of your University is now the object of derision, is now pointed at by the finger of scorn, though the respectability of his character be absolutely essential to the well-being of the great society which he governs. The Provost of your University thus publickly acknowledges, that he solely relies on the success of this appeal, on the strength of his defence, on the justice of his countrymen, for the recovery of his dignity: He, therefore, again repeats, this subject is of importance; he, therefore, again conjures the publick to give it their serious attention.

The adopting and executing a well-concerted system of education for youth, the instilling in their tender minds (now susceptible of those impressions which are to stamp their future character) the true principles of sound morality, solid learning, and legal liberty, have been ever and justly esteemed most highly interesting to the welfare of every well-regulated state; for, by such a prudent and effective discipline the members of those states will become valuable and virtuous citizens. The incomparable Thucydides (an historian unrivalled in the justness and wisdom of his reflections, and in the depth of his political knowledge) observes, that the Spartan legislator favoured by the Delphic Oracle, from whose awful shrine he received the glorious epithet of *Godlike*, derived this immortal compliment for his illustrious system of *educatory* regulations. Thus historical experience, and our own private reflections, unite in imprinting on our minds this important truth, that no state, no society can possibly flourish

whilst

whilst inattentive to the momentous concern, of establishing a prudent plan of wholesome discipline, by which the members of *those* communities are trained to an habitual reverence for, and conformity to the laws, virtue, and morality. These general principles, thus established, can without the possibility of cavil be applied to this country.

But before I make any pertinent reflections on this great subject, which I have thus endeavoured to bring home to the hearts and understandings of my countrymen, give me leave to advance this incontrovertible maxim, that no system of education, however ably or wisely planned, can possibly be effective, unless the most uniform respect be paid to the man, to whose knowledge, prudence and discretion, the execution of that system is committed. Though the evidence of this proposition must extort universal assent, yet too true it is that artful and designing men have thrown the most illiberal imputations on my knowledge and abilities; imputations most fatal in their consequences, in as much, as they have induced both *fellows* and *lads* to withdraw every mark of decent politeness to me. The *freshmen* laugh at me; the *fellows* brow-beat me; my public speaking is ridiculed; my public compositions are criticised. Let me calmly ask, is it fitting, that the Provost of a college should be causelessly made the butt of ridicule, the object of contempt? I cannot become the trumpeter of my own praise, I detest egotism: I do, however, appeal to the justice of my countrymen

countrymen (and confident I am, that this appeal cannot be attributed to vanity, the foible of weak and unmanly minds) I appeal to their veracity, whether many of them cannot, from their own experience give the lie to *those* ungenerous calumniators. I conjure my countrymen in the voice of truth, of reason and humanity, to controvert and oppose *those* dangerous falshoods: If, my friends, you regard your country, suffer not *those* fatal prejudices against, and this contemptible opinion of me, to take inveterate root, and to grow up in the minds of credulous boys. If any of you have influence within these walls, exert it without delay; assume the friendly office of mediators; represent me as a man, who would wish to treat the lads with the tenderness of parental affection, the fellows with the confidence of equal friendship; dispel if possible, the cloud of contempt which prevents my rising; you will thus facilitate the execution of my new regulations which will render this university the envy and the boast of Europe. This naturally leads me to a material observation; at the same time give me leave to assert, that I scorn, (if I may be indulged in the allusion) to pluck the laurel from the tomb of my predecessor, in order to form a wreath for my own brows; however my regard to truth compels me thus publickly to declare, though a regard for his memory would induce me to suppress, his scandalous inattention to the great duties of his office; and I give it as my opinion, that had he lived four years longer, science and learning must have

died,

died, and the banished muses mourned for ever. I hope my countrymen will excuse this digression; I hope they will see as clearly as I do, the necessity and importance of it. I will now enter into the justification of my conduct; but before I go fully into the subject, I could wish to lay before the public the real motives which influenced me to accept the provostship. I do solemnly aver, that I will not falsify, but that I will strictly adhere to the truth. What I have to say on this head must be deferred until my next publication: as the public well know to whom they are to attribute my fictitious name, I shall still subscribe myself

MODERATOR.

No 19.   *Friday, January* 13, 1775.

Atque utinam aut verus furor ille aut creditus esset.
OVID.

To the PT.

YOUR second address to the public has come to my Perusal, and merits some degree of notice. It deserves consideration, not on account of

its

its ftile, for it is inelegant; nor on account of its matter, for it is frivolous; but it deserves confideration becaufe it exhibits a lively proof of the impopotence of ingenuity, when employed on the fide of falfhood, in oppofition to truth. Your warmeft partizans allow, that language is your Forte. Not hardy enough to contend for the folidity of your judgment, they reft your merit on the elegance of your declamation, fatisfied in giving up the ftrong powers of your mind in return for the admiffion of polite eloquence;—and indeed they are right. Your moft vigorous efforts could never claim any pretenfion to the one, and your laft effay demonftrates you are but periodical in the other. I fhall not obferve minutely on your addrefs, for to be minute when the whole is but a tiffue of littlenefs, would be to make the comment as contemptible as the text. The pompous commencement of your letter led the publick to expect mighty things. A performance prefaced with all the big fplendour of importance, induced people to look for fomething beyond the mere play of words; for fomething which, though it fhould not raife admiration, might prevent difappointment. They hoped, through the fhallow clearnefs of the ftream, to difcover fomething like common fenfe at the bottom; but how were thofe expectations difgraced, when they read a laboured attempt at vindication, that did *not* vindicate; when they beheld a *Provoft* of a learned feminary, pedantick without learning, and verbofe without ftile! As to your giving the title of " incomparable"

comparable" to *Thucydides* in the midft of a long paffage, evidently calculated to eftablifh a comparifon between that judicious writer and yourfelf, I fhall not dwell on it. I will not cavil on trifling inconfiftencies. Indeed there is no neceffity where the *Provoft* is in queftion. I admit that " no fyftem of education, however ably or wifely planned, can be effective unlefs refpect be paid to the man to whofe execution the fyftem is committed ;" but before refpect is *paid*, it muft be *deferved*; and how refpect can be deferved by the mercenary drudge of a long feries of corrupt adminiftrations, the ingenuity of a *Hutchinfon*, only can explain. And how with fuch pretenfion it can be expected, the blufhing modefty of the fame gentlemen only can determine. You complain that " illiberal imputations have been thrown on your knowledge and abilities ; that therefore the *fellows* and *lads* are not decently polite to you." And do you ferioufly think that illiberal imputations can be fatal to real knowledge, and real abilities ? that they can be fatal to imputed knowledge and imputed abilities, the treatment you repine at clearly illuftrates. I admire your exclaiming againft Egotifm after you have juft declared that your meafures are dictated by wifdom, and founded on virtue. To exprefs deteftation for a thing almoft in the very act of doing it, is a figure of fingular boldnefs ; it has to recommend it what your integrity will have, whenever you chufe to pleafe the public with the glofs of Novelty. I am, with you, of opinion, that
" vanity

"vanity is the foible of unmanly minds;" of course it cannot possibly be a foible annexed to your constitution, that has given through life so many shining proofs of a manly spirit. Your calling out to all persons who have any influence within the college walls, " to exert it without delay;" presents a remarkable instance of elevation without dignity of station, without respect. You seem determined to spare neither the quick nor the dead. What had poor ANDREWS, to do with your whining appeal to the public? Living, he held you in avowed contempt. As you did not shew the resentment of a man *then*, you ought not to act a blacker part than ZANGA *now*; for even he " warred not with the dead;" but the grave is not sacred from the malignity of a coward, *Andrews*, with many positive faults, had some positive virtues. He could be an active faithful Friend; he could be zealous without being venal. The warm soil of his constitution threw up some plants that were vigorous, and not unwholsome. The spewy coldness of yours can nourish nothing but frigid poisons; but I will neither insult the memory of departed frailty, nor flatter the partiality of worthless petulance, by comparing a dead *Andrews*, with a living *Hutchinson*.

ANTI-MODERATOR.

No. 20.   *Monday, January* 16, 1775.

Nugæque canoræ.   Hor.

TO THE PUBLICK.

IT makes me extremely happy that the coincidence of law and college vacation puts it into my power to enter fully into my defence—into the merits of this *important* subject. The man arraigned at the awful bar of the publick is called on to defend himself;—he should not claim, from his rank, or from his station, an exemption from this duty.

But before I enter into the particulars of my defence, permit me to expose the restlessness of the malice of my enemies:—they have stiled (could this be credited even in the legends of scandal?—) my late publick addresses *verbose nonsense*, and *frothy declamation*. I scorn to refute this idle calumny: suffice it to say, that I *laboured* in their composition. In short, (if I may be indulged in the allusion) the foul magician, *Envy*, has raised up, and blackened my character, as a man, as a father, as a writer,

and

and as a speaker;—the knight-errants of the quill have eagerly pursued this phantom. I may, however, without vanity, assert, that after they had hunted it through every field of quibble, and every circle of chicane, they found it invulnerable.

I must now, to fulfil my promise, mention the motives which induced me to accept the provostship. I respect truth, and therefore will not swerve from it in this most solemn declaration—that neither avarice nor ambition influenced my conduct—that I was actuated by an irresistible passion for an easy, honourable literary retirement—that I was impelled, from a sincere regard for the interests of this great seminary, in which I received the rudiments of my education, to step forth to cherish, foster, and improve it:—yet what is my requital?——I have been called a *mean intruder*,—every opprobrious epithet that rancour could suggest has been unsparingly accumulated on me. Must not this short, unadorned recital draw tears from the eyes, and excite pity for my sufferings in the relenting breasts of my generous countrymen?—I shall leave this digression, (which I presume was not impertinent) and enter into my defence.

Give me leave, in the first place, to assert, that the college *ought* to be the provost's borough;—and though this be a concession which I might reasonably demand from my adversaries, yet I will demonstrate this truth---I will remove even the possibility

bility of cavil---I will eſtabliſh it on ſuch a foundation, that the *pickaxe* of ſophiſtry, the darts of humour, ſhall be unable to ſhake it. I muſt entreat my countrymen to turn their attention from the theory of, to the practice in our excellent conſtitution; and I now reſt my cauſe on this ſingle point. If one ſolitary inſtance can be produced in this or in the ſiſter kingdom, wherein a returning officer, lawfully veſted with the abſolute and unlimited nomination of the electors, did not claim and exert the right of appointing the repreſentatives, I give up my argument, and reſign all pretenſions to legal or conſtitutional knowledge. It is indiſputable that our ſtatutes have given me a poſitive power of appointing every and each elector; and therefore, by that grant, I am, in reaſon, in juſtice, and in right, intruſted with the ſole and excluſive privilege of chooſing the repreſentatives of the univerſity. Though this reaſoning be concluſive, and carries with it (in my mind) deciſive weight; yet, to put the matter paſt doubt, I will mention the invariable election rules of the univerſities in the ſiſter kingdom. The heads (I am not certain whether they are called provoſts) name the candidates to the electors, who conſtantly acquieſce in the judgment of their governors, and never interfere except in the mere act of giving their votes.—This, my countrymen, is an appeal to your experience and common ſenſe;---let my adverſaries meet me on this ground.

Permit

Permit me now to give the publick my most solemn assurance, that, from the strongest conviction and most mature consideration, I entertain this opinion--an opinion not lightly taken up, but founded on precedent and reason—that I am bound, in conscience and in duty, that it is my duty, as provost, as a servant of the crown, as a lover of my country, to exert those legal powers with which the constitution of the kingdom, and the statutes of this society have armed me, in effecting the return at the approaching election, of two men who obtain (and therefore merit) my approbation. I will thus preserve inviolate the great prerogative of my office---I will thus consult the dignity of the crown and of parliament, the welfare of this society, and happiness of the kingdom. Why, then, should I be ashamed to avow, that my conduct and my measures, since my appointment tended to *this single object*---the rendering this respectable corporation the provost's borough?---Let my base traducers blush, whose slanderous and venomous writings have made me the object of contempt and detestation---who have misrepresented that conduct which should endear me to my fellow citizens, and procure me the veneration of my country.——Excuse this warmth—the treatment I have met with extorted from me these opprobrious epithets—the dignity of my character, and the moderation of my temper, shall restrain any further expression of resentment—let their own feelings be their punishment.

Having

Having undeniably demonstrated that my actions have been founded on virtue, be it my part now to prove that they have been directed by wisdom, and were the result of prudence. I always imagined that the poor merit of consummate address was, by general consent, ascribed to me: yet even this part of my character has been attacked.

It would take up too much to enter into particulars at present: let me, however, conjure your attention for a few minutes to one striking fact.

It is well known that I have been ridiculed by the scribblers of the day, for calling nine boards, on an anonymous publication under the signature of *Verax**. I assert that this was a master-stroke in election-address. It was surely material to impress the members of the board with the highest respect for my abilities; for every man of common sense must see that I would thus effectually prevent their intended opposition to my collegiate regulations, as provost—to my parliamentary views, as returning officer. How could this be effected?—I knew that *those* gentlemen did not attend the Four-Courts or house of commons;—I therefore eagerly embraced this opportunity of displaying my critical and oratorical abilities;---I pointed out the inaccuracies in the stile of that composition;---I proved the advantages of the liberty of the press;---I demonstrated

* See No. 4.

monstrated the danger from its degeneracy into licentiousness;---I stated and obviated Lord Chesterfield's objections to a moderate restraint of it;---I introduced my *panegyrick* on *George Faulkner*;---I enforced my reasoning;---I delivered my poor sentiments with all the *energy* and *pathos* which this great subject should naturally call forth;---and was proceeding, at my ninth board, to lay before them a sketch of an excellent bill (which I have in contemplation) for preventing the abuse of this inestimable privilege---the boast of our enviable constitution---when I perceived (I glow with indignation while I relate it) that doctors Kearney, Wilson, and Murray, had fallen asleep.

Before I deduce my conclusion from the proceeding in general, give me leave to make one short observation on the gothic behaviour of these *inelegant Book-worms*;---the epithet may be thought too severe;---I will not, however, retract it, because they merit it. If I may be indulged in this pleasantry, they resembled the asses in the Italian fable on whom Morpheus sheds his poppies, whilst the nightingale sings.---But, to return to the subject, my particular observation is this: Is not the wisdom and penetration of our *excellent* chief governor; is not the parental affection to his people of the *best* of princes now clearly evidenced in their appointing me provost?---I may, without the imputation of self-conceit, assert that no man in the kingdom is better qualified for wiping away the rust necessarily contracted

tracted in scientifick ells.—My general conclusion is this: Could human wisdom (let me appeal to gentlemen's candour) suggest any scheme more likely to effect the end I had in view, than the conduct which I pursued at *those* boards?——It is not in a man's power to command success.—I shall now conclude with observing, that my calumniators have (to use an allusion) violated the laws of their country;— they have put my conduct to *the rack*;——be it my office to reunite its mangled limbs; to restore not only its firmness, but its beauty.

MODERATOR.

P. S. The p——t having, now, compleatly justified himself as to College-matters; will, in his next paper, address himself, particularly, to his respectable constituents.

No. 21.   *Wednesday, January* 18, 1774.

*Sit quoque nostra domus vel censu parva vel ortu,
Ingenio certe non latet illa meo.*   OVID.

TO THE RESPECTABLE ELECTORS OF THE
CITY OF CORKE.

IF the man who has sacrificed every private consideration—who has devoted his life to the service of his king and country—who has worn out his constitution, who has injured his fortune, by his unwearied attention to the interests of the publick—may, with propriety, claim from any set of men living a patient and unprejudiced hearing, whilst he refutes those calumnies from which his publick merit and his private virtues could not shield him, he surely might demand this small favour as his right, when he addresses himself to men who have long known and proved his worth—whose city, not long since a mere nest of smugglers, his poor efforts, zealously exerted, have raised to an enviable height—to men, who, with an honourable liberality of mind, must confess that they have now become, chiefly through his means, fair, respectable, and opulent traders. Your faithful representative, with a confidence

dence which conscious integrity could alone inspire, appeals to you, his constituents——to you submits the canvass of his conduct. Happy am I, in feeling that I must have, on this great occasion, a powerful advocate in your breasts—your gratitude. Is there an individual in your city who must not confess, that from me, in a great measure, he derives his comforts and his wealth?—Such services, I well know, might probably have out-tongued the clamours which prevail against me; and I might, without any imputation, have declined this species of justification, which some may think derogatory to my dignity. I can, however, claim, in this part of my conduct, the merit (merit by no means inconsiderable) that I have uniformly shewed the most respectful attention to you, my friends and fellow-citizens.

Permit me to remind you of what I have done, and what I have suffered for you. When his Majesty was pleased to confer on me the important trust of the provostship, I seized the earliest opportunity of communicating to you (and let me say this was a mark of respect which any other man in my situation would have omitted) the interesting intelligence of this honourable promotion. I wished too that your happiness on this occasion should not be in the least allayed; and therefore resolved that the tidings of this great event should be first announced to you *by my pen*. In a sentimental intercourse between delicate and warm friends, no mediator should be admitted;—the delightful stream of a mutual communication of thoughts should flow direct. For the sole purpose, therefore, of preventing a premature conveyance to you of the news of my appointment, I briskly pushed about (if I may be indulged in the pleasant allusion) an honourable falshood, and made my friend *Damer*, my *Croupier*: I made this *obliging* little man assert, in every quarter of the city, upon his honour, that I would not be so ungenerous as to solicit—that government would not be so wicked—as to grant me, this office. By this innocent contrivance I added considerably to the rapturous satisfaction of men, whose refined feelings so well qualify them for enjoying the delightful feast of friendship.

But exquisite sensibility has its misery.—I must wound your sympathetick breasts, when I tell you that appointment has embittered every hour of my life;—when I unbosom myself to you, in the confidence of friendship, and confess that the Provost's chair, in which I fondly hoped to repose myself, after the fatigues of a busy, bustling life, is a seat of thorns. And for whose sake have I suffered the miseries which my acceptance of the provostship has drawn on me?—For the sake of you, and your children;—an unremitting attention to your interests is the general spring of my actions, and solely influenced my conduct in this instance. From the day of my appointment I had resolved, in the discharge of the great duties of my important office, to

shew

shew such an exemplary attention to the learning and morals of your sons, that every father in your city must be branded as ungrateful, must be a bankrupt in honour, who did not repay *these* favours by an absolute surrender to me of the disposal of their votes.—Besides, I confess, I did once flatter myself that the influence within *those* walls necessarily derived to me from my station, must have enabled me to nominate the representatives of the university.— What advantages might I not then have reasonably expected to have procured for your city? With the addition of two or three members to my *following* in parliament, I should have effectuated schemes which would have rendered Corke the grand Emporium of the Universe.

I have not room in this, my first address to my constituents, to lay before them the important services which I have performed for them. I shall confine myself to the lighter though material obligations which they have received from me. At this period, when representatives presume to contemn the approbation, and slight the advice of their constituents in matters which particularly relate to them, what has been my conduct even on occasions in which they were not at all interested? I was basely calumniated, as having acted unconstitutionally in dispersing the meeting of the scholars. Did I by my silence countenance and encourage such attacks? Did I shew a contemptuous indifference to the good opinion of you, and the rest of my countrymen?—No;—the very next paper produced my refutation.

refutation under the same signature I now adopt; *
and the strong brightness of truth beaming forth
from that defence flashed conviction upon the minds
of gentlemen, who perused it. Did I trust to the
usual conveyance of news papers? Did I not send
my composition under cover to every respectable
constituent; every respectable gentleman in your
county? Did I not consult your commendable
frugality, a virtue, the basis of that hospitality
which characterises your city? And, did I not,
therefore, procure the Secretary's franks?———This,
my friends was a series of respectful attention, which
I will be bold to say, *no other* man in the kingdom,
circumstanced as I am, would have pursued.

When I was traduced in my collegiate character,
did I not discover the same praise-worth sensibility,
the same virtuous solicitude for your good estimation?
I summoned a board, I conjured the senior
fellows, as a suppliant, for a *certificate of my conduct*;
and, when *those* gentlemen opposed me, and asserted
that I was foregoing my dignity, I conjured
them in the pathetick voice of pity to grant my request.
They at length indulged me. Here let me
observe, that the difficulties I had to encounter in
this business enhance my merit. Did I, my fellow
citizens, rest my cause even on this justification?
No;—I wrote a pamphlet ‡ on my conduct, dispersed
it with my own hands in this, and sent it down to

* See No. 3. ‡ See No. 26.

your city —And here let me point out the great purposes of that pamphlet: first, it will aid me to recover my lost respectability of character, which should, I may say, be an inherent quality in the governor of this great society; and, secondly, it will serve as a model of composition. You may observe in perusing that pamphlet, that the great object of my new regulations is, to encourage that important art I have often lamented and admired that this great country, in which liberty, the nurse of genius, has fixed her seat, cannot boast of even one decent writer. When I anxiously turned this subject in my thoughts, I imputed the dearth of merit in this important branch of literature, to the want of an English standard in composing; and for this reason, because I well knew the natural indolence of my countrymen prevented their recurring to the great sources of antiquity, I thought it therefore my duty to engage in a course of laborious study; I read with intense attention, and with difficulty conquered those master writers (if I may use the expression) Thucydides and Demosthenes peri Stephanou. I transfused their majesty, their correctness, and their beauty, into the composition I allude to. In my style, I aimed at accuracy without prolixity, dignity without bombast, simplicity without meanness, and chastity without (if I may be indulged in applying the idea to composition) *prudery*. I endeavoured to make that poor piece, as all-bounteous nature has formed your daughters, fair, yet unadorned; elegant, yet unaffected.

unaffected. Above all things I took care to be correct without the disagreeable fault of *grammatical stiffness*. Thus, my friends, my labour and my time have been expended for the service of your children, for the service of the rising generation.

It pains the man who possesses a generous mind, to recite conferred favours. I must, however, point out to the principal merchants an obligation which they received from me. On my first introduction to them I perceived, during our festive intercourse, that they were *perfectly illiterate*. This misfortune could not be imputed to them; it must be ascribed to the contracted system of a commercial education. Anxious to contribute, as much as in me lay, to to their perfection, I made interest with government to be generally appointed for the Munster circuit. I thought that from the bench of justice, I could, with the most correct delicacy, instruct them in those common principles of legal knowledge and civil policy which every gentleman should know. Call to your minds my speeches to your grand jury. Did I not lay before them the origin of civil society? did I not distinguish and explain the different forms of government?——Did I not paint in glowing colours, with the pencil of a master, the outlines of our excellent constitution?—I will be bold to assert that no *other* judge in his majesty's dominions would, without reward, exert his powers of oratory for the space of four hours;

hours; and for no other purpose, but to instruct the ignorant.

I shall, with the greatest respect, take my leave for the present, and conclude with making this earnest request, that you will preserve each particular paper until the whole of this laborious, though necessary task be compleated: then read with candour, and with attention the system of my justification, and acknowledge I have raised such a fabrick of solid reasoning, and irrefragable defence, that every future attack of my enemies shall prove impotent.

MODERATOR.

No. 22.   *Friday, January 20, 1775.*

*Neve mihi noceat quod vobis semper, Achivi,
Profuit ingenium : meaque hæc facundia, si qua est,
Quæ nunc pro domino pro vobis sæpe locuta est,
Invidia caret.*   OVID.

TO THE RESPECTABLE ELECTORS OF THE CITY OF CORKE.

THIS is the important crisis of my life.——— Each hour presents new difficulties———new distresses. If such be my situation, I should pay an ill compliment to my generous constituents, in apologizing for this desultory (now the only possible) mode of justification. Perplexed, embarassed, uncounselled, unfriended, I must make this last appeal to the humanity of my countrymen; I must conjure their serious attention for the great purpose of candid disquisition. But before I enter into the grand question, permit me to defend my conduct on a late memorable occasion ‡. The practice of fighting duels I have ever abhorr'd, and heretofore ever avoided. I appeal to Mr. Devonshire for the truth of this last assertion. I appeal to my countrymen, whether my conduct in an affair of honour

‡ A few days before the publication of this paper, the provost fought Mr. Doyle.

with a deceased popular patriot did not evince the peaceableness of my disposition. The most respectable members in the house of commons can testify, that I always shewed, by my conduct in that assembly, a firm disinclination to the inhuman Gothick appeal. From the clearest principles of reason, I have formed this opinion, that an experienced senator, a faithful and able counsellor to his majesty, a virtuous representative, materially injures his country, his king, and his constituents, if he exposes his life in a foolish, unimportant dispute. There occur, however, in this earthly pilgrimage, some severe trials, wherein a man must desert his principles and do violence to his nature. In this light my countrymen will consider my late affair of honour, when I prove to demonstration, and force the most unreasonable man alive to confess, that I could not have declined that dreadful meeting, without submitting to the brand of a liar or a coward. Permit me to recite the facts truly as they were.—I unguardedly denounced vengeance against Mr. Doyle—I threatened to chastise him. You will credit this solemn asseveration, that I never intended to have executed these threats—that I never dreamed that those few idle words could have reached his ears: yet he did hear my declarations, and demanded satisfaction. Let me appeal to gentlemen's candour, could I have denied my assertions?——Could I have confessed myself a coward and a bully?——In this choice of difficulties, I was forced to adopt the resolution of accepting this gentleman's invitation to the
field

field of honour. Can any man come forth, and point out how I could have avoided this measure? If no man can, I must surely stand acquitted in the opinion of the great society which I govern, in the opinion of the great city which I represent. There is one important advantage which I shall probably derive from this transaction: gentlemen will now see that men of honour and of spirit will insist on atonement for abusive language; and since I can rightfully claim no inconsiderable rank in that respectable class, I might reasonably expect that the coward, foul-mouthed slander will henceforth close his lips. I warn, gentlemen (and surely the admonition must be acknowledged seasonable since party-rage daily sacrifices the most dignified characters at the altar of censure) that I will insult no man, and must not be insulted; that I will menace no man, and must not be menaced; that I will nickname no man, and must not be nicknamed. The criterion of a man of true honour is not to give nor to bear an affront. My expressing such sentiments might perhaps make some gentlemen in your city; (I allude to no man in particular) *really quake*. †

I shall now leave this necessary digression, and introduce the great subject of my address.—But before I enumerate the important advantages which you have derived from me—the important services which I had in contemplation to have performed for
you,

† Mr. Strettle, of Corke, is a Quaker.

you, give me leave to mention one striking instance of the most respectful and disinterested attention to your city and its citizens. I have selected Dr. Forsayeth as my favourite, my election-agent, and my adviser.—— This ruinous compliment has involved me in inextricable difficulties.——You all know the roughness of manners your townsman possesses, the violence of his temper, his perfect ignorance of the world and of the human heart.——Anxious to oblige you, yet dreading the effects of his intemperate zeal, I was reduced to the most distracting alternative. In this perplexed and pitiable state of mind the only expedient that occurred was, to recommend to him a cautious and attentive perusal of lord Chesterfield's letters. One difficulty started up—a suspicion I entertained of the soundness of the doctor's principles. I observed in him a perseverance in throwing illiberal imputations on the morals and knowledge of every tutor in the college, one excepted; as if the ruin of every other man's character was the only foundation on which he could erect the reputation of his friend. Dreading, therefore, the consequence of putting such an author into his hands, I thought it my duty to take him to my study; I there conjured him to arm himself with the shield of religion and morality against the dangerous attacks of the ingenious, noble libertine. But, alas! my admonition did not succeed. This fatal book has ruined his morals without polishing his manners. I have, however, procured him no inconsiderable confiderable preferment,† and folemnly promife that I will exert all my intereft to place a mitre on his head.

Thus far it appears, that I have on all occafions fhewed the moft punctilious refpect to you; my important fervices muft now be enumerated. I conceive that the great duty of a member of parliament is, to unite the interefts of the place he reprefents, and of the country in general. Has not this been my conduct? When our treafury was rich, when our refources were great, when there was an unapplied redundancy in the public coffers, did I not then procure for your city confiderable parliamentary bounties? But, when his gracious majefty was pleafed to defire that the money, which was formerly expended in the improvement of this country, fhould, in future, be devoted to the rewarding of his faithful fervants in the houfe of commons, did I from that period folicit the fmalleft grant for your city? No; my moft implacable enemies dare not affert it. I wifh for the profperity of your city; but, to promote it, I never will injure the kingdom. If the real wants of government, if the high official ftation I hold among the fervants of the crown, obliged me to affift in increafing the penfion and the place eftablifhment, the more obvious was the neceffity of my defifting from applications in behalf of your city; fince the confequence of their fuccefs muft have been the impofing of new taxes, or depriving

† The living of Kilcock.

priving the steady and warm supporters of administration of their well-earned stipends. How much, then, must this pleasing reflection increase your happiness; that your city has been improved with money, for which there was no other claimant; that you (if I may be indulged in the allusion) *flourish*, without having contributed to blast your neighbours. This too, must considerably add to your satisfaction, that many of my zealous *friends* (particularly that respectable citizen, Mr. Izod, to whom I am so nearly allied) have been rewarded by me with genteel and lucrative appointments in the expenditure of these publick grants.

This part of my subject naturally leads me to point out to you an instance of the most delicate respect that, perhaps, ever was observed by a representative to his constituents. When my imprudent colleague contributed 500 l. to the compleating your favourite walk, what was my conduct? I appeal even to my enemies, whether they can produce one instance of my ever having affronted the most opulent traders in his majesty's, or any other potentate's dominions, by offering my paltry private contributions to assist the effectuating of their great publick works?——No; I never will wound the honourable pride of a liberal merchant.

Has my attention to your interests been solely confined to the present hour? No;—I have enlarged the great and useful schemes I had conceived, ed, and extended my views to future ages. Conscious that I could easily have rendered my affection for your city hereditary, and that my sons, and son's sons would display the same ability and zeal in protecting your rights and in improving your trade, which you ever experienced in me, I had resolved to make your city a family-borough. For this purpose, I made several of my stauncheft friends free of your corporation, and attempted to confer this distinguished honour on a number of my tenants. But, you nourish vipers in your bosoms; you have friends in your city that were base enough to oppose (from selfish motives) and defeat the man who consults your interest and your honour.

Such have been my actual services;—such my intentions in your favour. Permit me now to address you, not in the rough language of an insolent blusterer, but in the gentle murmurings of a slighted lover to his mistress.———Was it not unkind to refuse me the common compliment of a civil address? I will venture to affirm (if I may be indulged in pursuing the metaphor) that I have no rival in your good graces who can boast of such constancy or warmth of affection. The good offices I have done you might, surely, have claimed so small a requital. Let me, however, assure you that no injuries, no insults shall abate my desire to serve you.

Here I must lament the disagreeable necessity which lord Shannon's coalition with government has imposed.

imposed on me. I am obliged to join interests with this nobleman. He artfully procured the intercession of our excellent chief governor. Gratitude induced me to comply—This will, surely, plead my excuse with men who, I hope, respect that virtue. It grieves me that this unfortunate junction has precluded the execution of a scheme honourable and beneficial to your city. When I imagined that I was unanimously to be elected your representative, my ardent gratitude for this distinguished compliment induced me to investigate, in the circle of my acquaintance, a man whose political sentiments I approved;—on whose honour I might rely for co-operating with me in the important guardianship of your interests.———Influenced by these motives, I should have proposed, as the second object of your choice, a friend well entitled to your unanimous suffrages. If, however, the meanest voter had the slightest objection to my first nominee (so great is my desire to conciliate every individual in your city) I would patiently submit to his unreasonable opposition, and chearfully withdraw my favourite. I should, however, have persevered in my duty; I should have persisted in recommending to you, my colleague, until I had pointed out a man in whose character malice itself could not find a stain. My enemies will say that I disguise selfish and private views, under the veil of public-spirited professions.——Observe, my friends, such a charge carries absurdity on the face of it.——It is well known that the parliamentary influence I must necessarily posfefs, along with my poor fpeaking abilities, is fufficient to anfwer every private purpofe. I own, I ardently wifh to have a refpectable following in the next parliament, for the fole purpofe of giving weight to a remonftrance which I fhall urge at the foot of the throne. I will infift on my removal from the port of Strangford to the port of Corke. I muft fay, that even the loyalty I bear my fovereign, does not entirely reprefs fome little refentment which arifes when I reflect upon my late appointment. I have ably and faithfully ferved his majefty in the law, in the military, in the literary line. He has lately been gracioufly pleafed to ftation me in the revenue-department. † I muft, however, fay, he has not treated me with his ufual indulgence, by banifhing me to the north. He fhould not have expofed a body reduced to decrepitude in his fervice, to the chilling blafts of that ungenial climate. He fhould know that I never did—that I never will make a finecure of any employment entrufted to me. If my reafonable requeft be complied with, I fhall divide my time in attending collegiate and revenue duties; and I doubt not but that, from my intimate acquaintance with the code of commercial laws, I fhall be able to execute fchemes which will enrich the crown, and, at the fame time, eafe the fair and induftrious trader.

You

† Searcher, Packer, and Gauger of Strangford.

You have now before you the whole fyſtem of that conduct which I have obſerved, and intended to obſerve towards you;—judge of it with impartiality;--liſten not to the ſuggeſtions of deſigning men. If you review with candour and with attention what I have ably ſtated and urged to you, the artifices of my enemies (the friends of faction) can never miſlead you.

MODERATOR.

Ad Quintum Hirpinum.
Hor. Lib. II. Ode XI.

Quid bellicosus Cantaber, et Scythes,
Hirpine Quinti, cogitet, Adriâ
    Divisus objecto, remissas
    Quærere, nec trepides in usum
Poscentis ævi pauca : fugit retro
Lævis juventas et decor, arida
    Pellente lascivos amores
    Canitie, facilemque somnum.
Non semper idem floribus est honos
Vernis, neque uno Luna rubens nitet
    Vultu : quid æternis minorem
    Consiliis animum fatigas ?

Cur non sub alta vel platano, vel hac
Pinu jacentes sic temere, et rosa
    Canos odorati capillos,
    Dum licet, Assyriaque nardo
Potamus uncti ? Dissipat Evius
Curas edaces. Quis puer ocius
    Restinguet ardentis Falerni
    Pocula prætereunte lympha ?
Quis devium scortum eliciet domo
Lyden ? Eburna, dic age, cum lyrâ
    Maturet, incomtum Lacænæ
    More comam religata nodum.

No. 23.

No. 23.   Saturday, January 21, 1775.
   Ex noto fictum carmen sequar.   Hor.

   TO SIR JOHN BLAQUIERE, K. B.

WHAT's angry *Tisdal's* secret aim,
   What's now infatiate PRANCER's claim,
Stay, and forget at London;
Blaquiere, thy own preferment's sure,
Thy place and pension are secure,
   Although the nation's undone.
Unequal to the statesman's toil,
No more that body twist and coil,
   And keep good people fasting;
Enjoy the world e'en while you may,
The strongest frames, you know, decay,
   And thine's not made for lasting.

In your own fifteen acres laid
We'll scorn that busy factious trade,
   Which cits takes such delight in;
Though you inclose fifteen beside,
Cits will have room enough to ride,
   And W———sh enough to fight in.
There chase the thoughts of publick shame
(For flatt'ry does as well as fame)
   With burgundy and sherry;
There open all your Gallick store,
Fran——s shall go and fetch your whore,
   And Sc——t shall make her merry.
Let her beneath the beechen shade,
Though for far other dryads made,
   Laugh at the Dublin jury;
Like ravish'd Helen, blous'd her hair,
Her leg, like Spartan Virgin's bare;
   Her breast, like those of Drury.

No. 24.

No. 24.   *Monday, January* 23, 1774.

"Ἵππαρχον κρεμασας μαστιγωσον.

PLUT. in ANT.

TO HIPPARCHUS.

HAPPILY for mankind, even the unprincipled and base find utility in honesty. The greatest villain (if a prudent one) will not do wrong without good cause, nor hazard the numberless advantages derived from the confidence and esteem of his fellow citizens, except it be to attain some very signal profit.

To recommend moderation and justice to *Hipparchus*, from *virtuous motives*, were to betray ignorance of the world, and of *his character:* but the *meanest* understanding may see the expediency of calmness in oppression, and decency in corruption;---might I persuade him to lop a few luxuriances from his Tyranny, I should materially serve him, and not dis-serve the community.

It is difficult (Hipparchus would say impossible) to find a man who acts on virtuous motives; yet if we cannot make men upright, let us entreat them to be moderate, and wish them to be prudent. Want of principle makes a more hateful compound with *folly* than with *common sense*: the blunders of the foolish are often more fatal than the iniquities of the dishonest. Wretched are they who must digest the bitter fruits of corruption grafted on folly; who who must mark the incestuous union between absurdity and baseness, and endure not only the intentional direct inflictions of malice, but the casual and indirect ones of weakness.

You, Hipparchus, are now in the situation of an unlucky boy, who has clambered to a house-top, and clings, trembling at his own temerity, and expecting to roll over and over with giddiness: all you must now hope for, is to fall in decent silence.

Censure was loud on your predecessor;—he gave too much cause for the clamour. Your conduct has been his best eulogium and justification: he was ever accounted an able – from comparison with you, he may be called a virtuous, incorrupt governor. By measures more violent than any attempted by him, you have wantonly thrown yourself into difficulties, from which a miracle alone can deliver you – your acting with temper and prudence.

Your

Your administration exhibits a mass of *crude, unformed, suspended* projects;—not unlike a broken, showry sky, where clouds are driven in confused, unstable heaps, before the wind. It seems as if you accepted your present post merely to gratify *your enemies* (or the *friends* of *virtue*) with a sight of the irrevocable blunders and irretrievable perplexities of a wretched man, closing in *absurdity* a life of venality and corruption.

The following hints (believe me) will be more useful in extricating you from your distress, than the frantick counsels of the *intemperate*, miserable man who engrosses your ear.

You will have as many opportunities of exposing the want of learned attainments as you can reasonably desire;—seek not to multiply them by such violent methods as altering the plan of education in your dominions.—Restrain the parade and bustling activity of forward, blundering, assuming ignorance.———Check the overflowings of vanity, the submissive insolence, and the studied tediousness.——Veil yourself from hostile remarkers in modest reserve.———Be not blinded when the servile burn their incense before the gilded idol; nor think that the respect and praise paid to station and wealth, are extorted by address, genius, and learning.

Your political schemes will be too heavy for your management.—Seek not supernumerary difficulties

by

by literary plans, which can anſwer no end, but to gratify the vanity, and ſhew the folly of their author.—Do not convene your council, unleſs you have buſineſs more important than to ſhew your oratory;—vulgar ſpirits will hardly find an attonement for loſs of time and the vexation of debates, prolix as unimportant, even in the elocution of an Hipparchus.—The majeſty of power falls into contempt, when mighty efforts are tried, and *found inſufficient* to produce *trifles*;—when *preparation, ſolemnity* and *parade*, uſher in *nothings*;—when deliberation, conſultation, declamation, *written harangues*, and elaborate oratory end in projects (like their *projector) unweildy, lame, empty, ſolemn,* and *inſignificant.*

An attention to ſtrict diſcipline is ſurely commendable;—yet it may irritate prejudiced minds, who will call it the poor revenge of diſappointed tyranny, or a ſnare for untractable ſpirits, covered over with pretended zeal for the publick good.

Your care for religion is ſignal, and *ſuits your character:*—yet, in a man of leſs *exemplary piety,* it might be called an hypocritical endeavour to ſanctify miſdeeds, by pious grimace—an attempt to turn our eyes from *old* latitude of opinion, by new obſervances and punctualities—the complaiſance (exceſſive from a conſciouſneſs of its being inſincere) of a *Deiſt,* feigning reſpect for opinions and ceremonies at which he laughs in his heart—or a *proſane fane perverfion* of religion to the purpofes of tyranny, as an engine for harraffing the obnoxious.

As the generous fpirit of electors, aided by your own perverfe endeavours, muſt cut off all your hopes of influencing the election, if you are wife, you will not interfere where you cannot prevail: but a fcene for exercifing corruption is, perhaps, too ſtrong a temptation for a corrupt mind. Act, then, with moderation;—let your applications to individuals be as fecret as may be;—befiege the younger electors by their parents and connections—hold forth to them rewards;—ufe rather the emollients of mildnefs and civility, than the caufticks of threats and perfecution.

Should an individual, from whofe wants and neceffities you might well expect pliability, prove refractory, you will not dare to rob him of the little employment which he has difcharged without reproach, and which only the *council at large* can legally give or take away.—No! This is too bold an exertion of tyranny and cruelty, even for *your* unblufhing want of principle, and the *raſh malevolence* of your *faintly adviſer*.

† Let your fpies and emiffaries mix among your opponents;—endeavour to fow diffentions, and raife various fentiments among them;—divide and rule them. Affail the fuperior electors with flattery, convivial *pleafures*, and the condefcenfion of familiar

† *Hipparchus* has followed this advice.

familiar converse. Flattery is powerful;—from a superior, almost irresistible;—to an irresolute, bashful man, unacquainted with the world, the familiarity of the great is an inevitable snare;—his vanity rises to make the continuance of it valuable and necessary;—dazzled by the difference of rank, he thinks it a favour which can only be repaid by implicit obedience. A heart, at once confounded with religious reverence, on admission to the penetralia of greatness, awed by its own timidity, and opened by the festal moment, will make all your requests, commands. You will meet, however, with many spirits of a contrary stamp,; and in his conduct to these, I need not caution a *politician* to use temper and politeness—to check the overflowings of his native insolence and petulance—and not to insult whom he cannot persuade.

I now leave you to the difficulties you have created—to the opposition you must encounter—to the shame you must endure—to the disappointment that awaits you in another quarter. It may seem cruel to reproach bodily infirmities; yet they deserve remark, as aggravations of guilt, when men sin in despight of nature. There is an uncommon depravity, a strange hunger and thirst after corruption in him who employs the poor precarious remnant of days, *multiplied by art*, in multiplying offences; who, diffusing mischiefs, prolongs his being to prolong injuries to his country—and, within sight of the grave, meditates a dreadful legacy to *posterity* of meanness, baseness, and perfidy, in his example and influence.

CHARIDEMUS.

※※※※※※※※※※※※※※※※※※※※※

No. 25.   *Monday, January 23, 1775.*

Major Rerum mihi nascitur ordo.   Virg.

ANNUS MIRABILIS

A POEM.

Most humbly inscribed to the Right Hon. John Hely Hutchinson, *and dutifully offered as a* Prize-Composition *for his intended Premium.*

Sir,

WHILE *new born* schemes the fost'ring hand,
  Or *Embrio*, midwife arts demand;
While *Alma*'s honour you advance,
By verse, by eloquence and dance,
And form the youthful heel and tongue
To frisk in rigadoon, or song;—
May I, from boards and pleadings steal
An hour, (nor hurt the common-weal)
To sing how you adorn the college,
With new pursuits, and useful knowledge?

Each

Each cobler's stall shall hold your praise,
And ballad-singers chaunt the lays.
Say does the muse mispend her rage,
When signal actions fill her page?

To tell then, gentle maid! proceed,
How *Alma*'s sons are taught to *read*:
The well-grown masters—Graduates small—
And *Didymus!* biggest boy of all.
The *Great Man* courts, and law books scorning,
Bestows on them an Attick morning.
Patient attends—the horn-book holds;
And sometimes cheers, and sometimes scolds;
Corrects the brogue; the snuffle taxes:
The dullest youth a *Tully* waxes.

To raise our eloquence still more,
A noble scheme he has in store.
If aught futurity I'm skill'd in,
A *Theatre*, (a stately building!)
Beneath his auspices shall rise,
To glad our wond'ring ears and eyes:
Othellos there and *Lears* shall rage,
And *Hamlets* tread the buskin'd stage;
Be pretty lost *Ophelia* there,
The *Orphan-Bride* and *Belvedere*.
Alma the magick scene shall view,
And iron tears the stage bedew,
From many a grave professor's cheek,
Deep-furrow'd in the search of Greek.

Her

Her seven wise men, in gowns of rouge,
A senate form—their head, the *Doge*.
Her bell for *Pierre* shall *Alma* toll;
Her ale infuse in *Zara*'s bowl;
Her porters range, and bid them stand
Theatrick guards—a solemn band!

O! but I had almost forgot——
Here the *Four Kings* paid scot and lot,*
And dwelt old inmates of the place;
But soon you chas'd the wizard race;
Dread pains and penalties inflicted,
From *Fire* and *Water* interdicted;
Nor *Tea* nor *Coffee* shall they taste,
Nor near the *social Hearth* be plac'd.
You, bag and baggage, made them pack;
Old *Whist*, and *Slam* that saucy Jack,
Ombre, Quadrille, Pope Joan, Picquet,
And Brag, and Cribbage—cursed set;
All, all, our worthy chief sent packing,
And, lest amusements shou'd be lacking,
He set the college youth to dancing;
Now retreating, now advancing,
While sharp violins are heard around,
And bagpipes' merry, merry sound.

Go on, great Sir!—beneath your eyes
Sublime pursuits and aims shall rise;

* Alluding to the interdict of cards within the walls of the University; our worthy Provost having very properly enforced the statute made and provided against them.

For

For somersets be *Alma* known,
Be vaults and tourbillons her own.
—The mask where belles and courtiers lead,
Where lovers dance in flow'ry mead;
Where'er the sprightly heart is found,
That flutters at a fiddle's sound;
Wherever dwells the janty fair,
Who capers at a jiggish air;
Thy toils shall find a deathless name,
And *Alma*'s jigs be Hely's fame;
Restorer of the art of dancing,
And mighty prototype of *prancing*.

Illustrious Sir! your schemes pursue,
So great, so solemn, and so new.
Heed not the lewd and idle scoffer,
Who laughs when gravest projects offer;
And just his silly nose can pop
Into the *ridicule* at top,
That rises light and vain (I wot)
As froth upon a porter-pot;
But waits not *serious ends* to know,
That, like the liquor, lie *below*.

For *Slingsby* the professor's chair,
The *fellow*'s cap and gown prepare;
And let the cynick fool be told,
How *kings* and *heroes* danc'd of old;
Refer him to the classick tome,
For *Salian dance* in ancient Rome:

Or

Or on the *pyrrhick* shew your reading;
And clear to *day-light* the proceeding,
By *Scaliger*, of modern days,
Who set all Germany a-gaze.
Thus wake the youth of gen'rous soul,
To chalk his pumps, and wield the *pole*;
Bid *graduates*, pendent by their knees,
From *Slack-ropes* shoot into *Degrees*:
While thy paternal skill imparts,
To other students other arts;
While some it forms (no trivial care)
To stalk on hands, with legs in air,
To greener palms shall some aspire,
And tread, equilibrists, the wire;
Or tumblers, round on platters spin,
Or dart through holes, like Harlequin:
In armour shall *Ben Saddi* † prance,
And clash his shield in *pyrrhick dance*;
To stand on's head *Sir Billy* ‡ strains,
And thence the jumble of his brains;
With coat of motley on his back,
Shall *Mendax* strut, a Pudding-Jack; §
But noblest, who with artful grace,
A *table* on his *nose* can place.

† Dr. F———th.   ‡ Mr. H———s.

§ This gentleman excells in the manufacture of *black puddings*, as appears from a speech of his to the late Provost. "My dear Provost, I vow to the Lord, I was just salting a "parcel of black-puddings with my *own hands* to send you; "when I heard the news of my father's house being robbed."

But

But thee, more useful toils await,
O! may the Parcæ stretch thy date.
Thy labours then, to glad this isle,
Shall raise a vast and goodly pile.
The *riding-house* shall rear its head,
Soft, soft the *horse dung* shall be spread.
No more with squares and circles addle,
See half the College in the saddle!
The whip, the boot our youth demand,
Dust, not inglorious, stains the band.
Soon shall thy *Centaurs* claim the fight,
And *City Lapiths* own their might:
The tribes that forge the ductile brass,
Or puff to form the molten glass,
The factious clans that shuttles guide,
And butchers fell, in crimson dy'd.
Lanes, ‖ *earth* and *water* send in mud,
And shambles weep thy rage in blood.
The haughty corporations bend,
And golden box for tribute send.
Thus train thy bands to fighting fields,
And reap the palms thy valour yields.

With conquest flush'd, our puissant head
To new exploits his troops shall lead;
To raze th' obscene and loathly cells,
Where shrin'd in darkness *Slander* dwells.

‖ Among the ancients, the sending of earth and water from one state to another, was a token of subjection. See Thucydides, passim.

With mangled reputations fed,
That serve her for her daily bread.
Through *High-street* shall he proudly march,
To storm her fane at *Owens-arch*. †
Through *Newgate* then,—tremendous tow'r,
His doughty host to *Meath-street* pour.
There, there the din, the tumults rise;
In dust th' *Hibernian Office* lies;
The *Devils* are to atoms batter'd,
Types, papers, poems, presses scatter'd.
Their journal lost, no jealous fear
Shall rouse the men that *dye* and *shear*;
Their feuds with Blaquiere then shall cease,
And solemn *Simon* rule in peace.

One last exploit is doom'd by heav'n,
And then thy sword to rust be giv'n:
Far hence dull plodding *troth* to beat,
That loads too long *Astrea*'s feat;
To bear away the *Chanc'llor's* mace,
Fix thee triumphant in his place.
Then shall thy cares, thy toils be crown'd,
And *Io Pæans* ring around.

† The Freeman's-Journal is published there.

No. 26.   *Tuesday, January* 24, 1775 ‡.

Nil oriturum alias, nil ortum tale fatentes.   HOR.

I am the man that did the bottle bring.
And tied the bottle to the bottle string.
                              TOM. THUMB.

An ACCOUNT of some REGULATIONS made in Trinity-College, Dublin, since the appointment of the present PROVOST.

THE people of this kingdom, of almost every rank, are interested in the good or bad conduct of the head of this university ; some men may have their motives for applauding, but many may be stimulated by ambition, interest, electioneering policy, or prejudice, to misrepresent and censure his conduct ; the publick who have none of
those

‡ This defence of the ——— *written by himself*, is placed here merely because it ought to precede the several critiques that were written upon it. It was printed January 6, 1775, for A. Leathly, bookseller to the university, but not *published*. Two hundred copies, (we have been informed) were deposited in the shop of Mrs. Leathly, to be distributed *gratis*, but on the appearance of No. 27. they were all *recalled*.

those motives, should form their opinions from facts. They are here faithfully collected, and from a plain state of them, every reasonable man may judge, whether this College has, or has not, obtained any benefits, or received any improvements, since the appointment of the present Provost.

That composition and elocution were not sufficiently cultivated among us, has been generally acknowledged and lamented: the first object of the Provost was to encourage an attention to those long neglected subjects; for this purpose.—

He obtained from the governors of *Erasmus Smith's* schools, to which he is treasurer, a fund of 200*l* yearly, to be given in premiums for composition and elocution, at such times, and in such manner and proportion, as the Provost and senior Fellows, should from time to time appoint.

But as a foundation should be laid at school for those useful accomplishments, he proposed the following advertisement, which was afterwards published by order of the board:

" Whereas the right honourable and honourable
" the governors of *Erasmus Smith's* schools, have
" been pleased to grant the sum of 200*l* yearly, as a
" fund for premiums for compositions, in *Greek*,
" *Latin*, and *English*, and for elocution in *Latin*
" and *English*; to be distributed by the Provost
" and

"and senior fellows of this university in such man-
"ner as they from time to time shall think proper:
"The several school-masters and tutors, who pre-
"pare young gentlemen for the said university, are
"desired to take notice. That from the 7th of *July*
"next, compositions in *Latin* and *English* prose,
"and from the 7th of *July* 1776, in *Latin* verse
"also, will be expected, from the several candi-
"dates for admission, at their examinations for
"entrance; and that during the college course,
"judgments will be given, and premiums distri-
"buted, for composition in *Greek*, *Latin*, and
"*English*; the like encouragement will be given to
"elocution in *Latin* and *English*: of which notice
"is given, that there may be sufficient time for
"preparation."

He also applied to government to be pleased to give directions that letters should be written to the several schoolmasters, appointed by his majesty in this kingdom, to prepare their scholars in such a manner as to enable them to become proper candidates for *those* premiums; this request was complied with; as treasurer of *Erasmus Smith*'s schools, he has written letters of the like import to the several schoolmasters upon that foundation; and, at his instance, the schoolmaster of the school in *Kilkenny*, now in the patronage of the college, has been written to from the board, in the same manner.

He

He has also obtained from the said governors a sum of 2500*l.* towards building a theatre for our publick exercises and exhibitions, and for delivering such compositions of the students as shall be approved of by the provost and senior fellows, to be built in such part of the said college as the provost and senior fellows shall approve of, and as nearly as may be according to the plan of the *Oxford* theatre.

The board has, at his instance, agreed that such of the batchelors as thought proper should give in speeches to the senior lecturer, with or without names, for the 30th of January, 29th of *May*, 4th of *June*, 23d of *October*, and 5th of *November*, on which days occasional orations are annually made; that *those* speeches shall be laid before the board, that the best should be spoken, and the author of it receive a premium. *(a)*

He has directed the oratory professor and his assistant, the tutors, the morning lecturers, and the censor to select the best exercises given in to them, and to *hand them over* to him *to see* which of them deserve to be distinguished in the same manner.

A general

(a) Premiums in this college are given in medals, or in books, with the college arms, and a certificate of the cause.

A general scheme for the encouragement of composition and elocution, in the several classes, is now, at his desire, under the consideration of the board; and there appears to be a fair prospect of extending *those* important attainments more generally in this university.

Upon his proposal the board resolved, that it would be highly beneficial to have professors of modern languages, namely Spanish, French, Italian and German, established in this college; he has applied to government to grant a moderate fund for that purpose, and has declared his intentions, if that application fail, to give an annual sum of two hundred pounds, out of his salary as provost, for that useful purpose; he has also proposed, and the board has agreed, that there should be a riding-house in the college for the use of the students only. The two last mentioned schemes will be a great saving to this country, will be the means of enabling young gentlemen of fortune to finish their education at home, and will send them abroad more capable of receiving improvement from their travels, when they are acquainted with the languages of the countries which they visit.

These institutions will be attended with this further advantage:—The gentlemen of this university, who would accept of private tuitions, though several of them are now men of great learning and ability, would by *those* accomplishments be
rendered

rendered *more* useful to their pupils; *those* attainments may probably be powerful inducements to the nobility and principal gentry, to commit their sons to the care of *those* gentlemen, both at home and abroad; and it is well known what beneficial consequences are frequently derived to the tutors from such connexions.

Nor have the great branches of solid and useful learning been neglected for the cultivation of less important objects.

There are several professors in the college, of divinity, mathematicks, natural philosophy, Hebrew, oratory, and common law; some of them *founded* and *endowed* by the crown, others endowed by the governors of *Erasmus Smith*'s schools; all filled by men of great knowledge and ability, and some of them of as high characters as perhaps ever filled *those chairs* in any university; yet *those* professorships have been all of them less useful, and some of them of *little use* by the non attendance or the negligent attendance of several of the batchelors; this will be for the future prevented by a regulation proposed by the provost, and adopted by the board, obliging the batchelors to attend the lectures directed for that profession for which they have declared, and punishing them for not attending or for negligence, by private admonishment for the offence of the first term, publick admonishment for the second, and removal from the college for the third:

Their

Their diligence and good anfwering are to be encouraged.

Premiums were formerly, and are now, given to the divinity, and Greek *lectures*; it is determined, at his defire, to extend them to the Hebrew, hiftorical, oratory, and common law lectures.

For the latter it has been ordered that a good common law library fhould be purchafed, together with fome of the moft neceffary books for a lending library, and that a convenient room fhould be fet apart for that purpofe; the common law profeffor is to lecture twice in the week in each term, is to examine the gentlemen in the books they read, and to examine publickly once in the year, and the board are to give premiums in law books to the two beft anfwerers.

This lecture which has been hitherto of little, or no ufe in this univerfity, is now placed upon fuch a footing, as under the fuperintendency of the provoft, who propofes to affift in the yearly examination, and fometimes to prelect *and in the hands of the prefent able profeffor*, will make it a very great national benefit to this kingdom: three months in the year, at moft, will be fufficient to anfwer the four terms in England; the reft of the year may be moft ufefully employed by the law ftudents in this college under the law profeffor, and in endeavouring to improve and diftinguifh themfelves in compofition, elocution, and hiftory.

It

It is obvious, if this scheme succeeds, that it will be attended with a great saving to this country.

He has also proposed, and it has been determined, that the apparatus for making the experiments in natural philosophy shall be enlarged and compleated.

He is using his utmost efforts for making the offices of divinity lecturer and divinity professor more useful than they have been for many years past; and the best founded expectations are entertained that his endeavours in this respect will be attended with the most useful and important consequences.

The course of education for under graduates in this university, in the general so justly approved, has in the classical part, been complained of as defective in some particulars; it is now, after great deliberation, settled that such alterations and improvements shall be made in it as will be highly beneficial to the students of the four first classes; this improvement of the undergraduate course, and obliging the batchelors in their respective lines of studies to attend the professors of those branches to which they are to *apply*, will form as complete a system of education as any in Europe.

The number of students is now five hundred and ninety-eight; the buildings of the college contain two hundred and twenty-five only; this is a great
cause

cause of relaxation of discipline, as the officers of the college cannot be responsible for the conduct of those who live in town; to remedy this inconvenience, the provost has proposed and the board has agreed to the erecting new buildings which will form a square, each side of which will be about two hundred and twenty feet in length; *and three sides of it will be new*; this is to be begun immediately.

He has shut up all access directly from the town to the college park, which had become a publick walk, *and* frequently for company of the lowest and worst kind, *and was made a common passage*; it is now reserved solely for the students; and it has been resolved at his desire, that a field for their exercises shall be provided when it can be done with convenience.

He has also declared his intentions of providing common rooms for the accommodation of the gentlemen of the college; one for the fellows and graduates, the other for the undergraduates in the manner of Oxford and Cambridge, and as *those* rooms will be supplied with newspapers, tea, coffee, &c. it is hoped *it* may be the means, by making the college more agreeable to the students, of preventing them from going so very frequently into town.

In a great and numerous university, situate in a metropolis, discipline is a most important object; as such he has attended to it with the utmost care

and

and solicitude: a moderate but exact discipline is established; the statutable regulation of not going into the city without a written permission from the tutor, is strictly attended to; the number of tardes, or coming in too late for night roll, restrained and determined; a new provision has been made as to night rolls, which has already been attended with the most salutary effects; missing a third night-roll is now made punishable by publick censures, and a fourth, without a sufficient excuse, by removal from the college; *he has encreased and fixed the number of chapels in a week*, and Divine Worship was never known to be better attended in this college; he has abolished an improper practice that had prevailed of some of the students leaving chapel before the communion service *of* a sacrament Sunday.

For the purpose of enforcing discipline, he has made the place of senior dean an active and effective office; it is now filled by one of the most respectable senior fellows, and the office of junior dean, by one of the most respectable junior fellows; *those* gentlemen being of distinguished characters as disciplinarians, were prevailed upon at the earnest desire of the provost, to undertake *those* difficult and important offices; scholars are visited by *those* gentlemen in their rooms, and the tutors also are ordered to visit their pupils in their rooms, and at stated times at their houses in town, and no pupil is to be allowed to continue at any house not approved of by his tutor; in a word, nothing has been

been omitted that can enforce a mild and regular discipline, without rigor or severity.

All offences have been investigated with the strictest attention, and offenders punished, without exception or distinction, but with all the moderation and lenity that were consistent with justice to the university, and to the publick.

In the quarterly examinations which by the statutes are to be for eight hours, at least two hours were wasted in calling the rolls, which sometimes did not leave sufficient time to distinguish the different degrees of merit, and particularly of the candidates for premiums; he has ordered that the roll should be called but once, and that on the first morning *only, and to be finished* before eight o'clock, when the examination begins, which leaves the whole time appointed by the statutes for the purpose of examining the students.

The favours of the college have been disposed of with the most scrupulous regard to justice and good example; in the distribution of natives places and exhibitions, † a new mode was proposed by the provost and agreed to by the board. That every man's pretensions should be determined by considering,

† The first are salaries of twenty pounds yearly, to such scholars of the house as are natives of Ireland; and the second, annuities of different values from five pounds to ten pounds yearly.

ing, first, his attendance upon religious duties and his moral character; secondly, his judgments at examinations; thirdly, his attendance on lectures and other duties; fourthly, his marks at schorlarship, fifthly, his seniority; and sixthly, his poverty. In every division the whole academical conduct of every student was strictly reviewed, and every place disposed of with a religious attention to *those* different kinds of merit; which must be attended with the best consequences, as it will make every man, who feels for the favours of the university, attentive to every step of his conduct, which he knows will be minutely investigated and closely reviewed and considered.

He has attended with the utmost application and vigilance to every part of his duty, and to enable the college to accomplish the many great and extensive plans which he has proposed for its improvement and enlargement. He has set on foot a scheme, for a reasonable and moderate encrease of the revenues of the university, which will be necessary for attaining *those* many great and useful purposes.

Those are facts.——If any thing wrong has been done, let the fact be stated; if any thing necessary or proper to be done, has been omitted, let the omission be stated. The publick may be amused, but will not be misled by electioneering invectives and scurrility.

If

If this gentleman has been able to do so much in six months, what may not be expected in a course of years from his perseverance? *Those* persons are not friends to their country who endeavour to mislead the publick opinion, to poison the minds of the students, and enflame them against their governor, by the most false, wicked and malicious calumnies. The assistance of the able, learned and worthy men, who are at present at the board of senior fellows, does not diminish his merit, but their concurrence is a strong proof of the propriety of *those* measures, of the rectitude of his conduct, and of the integrity of his intentions; and the most perfect concord, and reciprocal esteem have uniformly subsisted between him and *those* gentlemen.

No. 27.

144   PRANCERIANA.

No. 27.   *Wednesday, January 25, 1775*

Parturiunt montes nascetur ridiculus mus.   HOR.

TO THE STUDENTS OF THE UNIVERSITY.

HAPPENING a few days since to go to the chambers of a class-fellow, who on account of his having taken a lead in the late political contests, has been marked out by the Provost, and in consequence been cited more than once before the board for I know not what offence, my eyes were attracted by a pamphlet which lay upon the table, and appeared just fresh from the press. On the outside, I perceived in large characters, which
I knew

I knew to be my friend's, thefe words:—*O that mine adverfary had written a book!*——And underneath,—*O Fortunatam natam, me Confule, Romam!*—I immediately took it up, and found it entitled, AN ACCOUNT OF SOME REGULATIONS MADE IN TRINITY COLLEGE, DUBLIN, SINCE THE APPOINTMENT OF THE PRESENT PROVOST. Having heard a good deal of the prefent College Difputes, though I am not much interefted in them (not being a fcholar of the houfe), my curiofity was naturally excited by the title of this performance, as well as by the *mottoes* which my friend had affixed to it; and I read it through with great avidity. On the firft glance it appeared evidently the production of our illuftrious *Pacha* with *three Tails*—the great MAN-MOUNTAIN himfelf; and on enquiry I found that feveral copies of this work had been fent to each of the *fellows*, and to all his friends in and out of the Univerfity.

If this fingular performance had been *publifhed*, I fhould have left the examination of it to my coufin STULTIFEX, whofe acute ftrictures have already fo often entertained the publick. But as it is only *privately* difperfed, and may therefore never fall into my kinfman's hands, I think it my duty to take up his pen, from the fame laudable motive by which he appears to be actuated,—a defire to refcue the literary character of Ireland from reproach, and to preferve our mother-tongue unpoluted by the depravations of vulgar, inflated, or ungrammatical writers.

H That

That corruption has pervaded every part of our constitution, has been so long complained of and lamented, that we now acquiesce in the position as an incontrovertible truth, and submit to it as to other irremediable evils.—But our *language* has hitherto escaped its baneful and wide-spreading influence; at least its purity has been preserved by the *literati* of England and Ireland; nor has any member of this university hitherto brought shame on the society and himself, by any publick and notorious inability to deliver his ideas to the world with perspicuity and precision.—So far, indeed, has our language been from depravation, that during these last thirty years it has undoubtedly been much improved; and we have an excellent grammar extant, by means of which any man (except Humphry Search, Brutus, or the marble-headed Knight) may, with a very little application, learn to write at least correctly, if not with elegance.—*That person therefore is not a friend to his country*, who lessens the reputation of the only seminary of learning in it, *and poisons the minds of the Students*, by exhibiting to them a base model of composition,—by corrupting the modes of speech, and the analogy of language.

Had the Provost confined our disgrace to this country, it would have been more tolerable; but in order to diffuse it as wide as possible, he has, we are told, sent several copies of his work to the great schools, and the two Universities of England, and one to his Majesty.—*Nostra per immensas ibunt præ-*
conia

conia gentes.—Thus it becomes a matter of national concern; and it is the interest of every gownsman, lest he should be involved in the opprobrium which will certainly fall on our University, to declare to the world, that he sees with concern the head of the only college in this kingdom, exhibit to the publick a composition replete with almost every anomaly that the English language affords.

With respect to the objects of the present Provost,—the converting the College into a family-borough, and the establishing of certain new institutions——as a lover of independency, and a friend to the constitution, I heartily hope he may be defeated in the former; as a member of the University, and a well-wisher to it, I shall be no less pleased that his new regulations, if they be well conceived, may be as happily executed.—To oppose him in the former, and to scrutinize the latter, I leave to others. To review his periods, and examine his diction, is a task sufficiently burthensome for a single person.

But before I proceed to review the language of this elaborate performance, I cannot forbear to take notice of the sophistry of the argument.—The electors of the University hear that the Provost has sent to several of the fellows, and solicited their votes for two persons whom he should name. They are immediately alarmed;—they meet—associate—and resolve to maintain their independence.—The Provost is enraged; the most violent measures are adopted;

dopted;—frequent boards are held; several scholars are cited, examined, threatened, censured. In a word, the contest is carried on (as far as I have learned) with firmness and moderation on one side, and much intemperance on the other.—Thus stands the matter.——And now for argument. " An unreasonable outcry has been made;——I have been calumniated;—I am wholly innocent; for (I know, gentle reader, you expect he should say, ' *I have been guilty of no violence,---I have not endeavoured to dictate representatives,---I have not invaded the rights of the electors*—but you are mistaken;')——I have made such and such regulations with respect to the discipline of the University, and they are all excellent."——In the name of *Smiglecius* does he think us totally devoid of common sense? Whether his regulations are wise, or not, time only can shew; but surely they are *nothing to the purpose:* and *every freshman* would tell him that his argument is not *ad idem*.

The first paragraph that attracts our notice, runs thus:

" These institutions will be attended with this
" further advantage:—The gentlemen of this University, who would accept of private tuitions,
" *though several of them are now men of great learning and ability*, would by those accomplishments
" (i. e. the *establishment* of professors of modern languages, and the *building* of a riding-house, for
" these

" these are mentioned immediately before) be ren-
" dered *more useful* to their pupils." [*An account,
&c. p. 5.*]

By this paragraph are we to understand, that these gentlemen would accept of tuitions, notwithstanding that they are men of abilities?—Or, that by these, I beg pardon, I should say *those*, accomplishments (*the professorships and the riding-house*) they would be more useful than without them?—Or, that *those* accomplishments are more useful than learning and ability?

It certainly requires a gloss;—and the learned writer will do well to add one in the next edition.

But let us hasten from these petty inaccuracies, to the most extraordinary piece of writing that we ever remember to have met with.

" There are several *professors* in the college of di-
" vinity, mathematics, natural philosophy, hebrew,
" oratory, and common law; some of them *founded*
" and *endowed* by the crown, others endowed by
" the governors of Erasmus Smith's schools; all *filled*
" by men of great knowledge and ability, and some
" of them of as high characters as, perhaps ever
" filled *those chairs* in any university." [*Ante
page* 136.]

Every one has heard of the founding of a school, or college;——but the *founding of professors* is quite new-

new. The present fellows of the University are men of acknowledged abilities, and, I am sure, are as loyal as any of his Majesty's subjects; but I much question whether they will allow that any one but God Almighty has *endowed* them with those faculties which they possess: nor, indeed, did I ever hear before that such a power as is here mentioned resided in the crown. But it seems that not only his Majesty, but the governors of Erasmus Smith's schools, for the time being, are gifted with this extraordinary power. They have acquired it, no doubt, since the appointment of the present Provost. But the matter does not rest here. *Those* professors are not only *endowed* by the crown, but they are *filled* by men of great knowledge and ability —— That *those* professors should, like the Trojan horse, carry *men* in their bellies, is no doubt, a wonderful phenomenon;—but as we must take it for granted, that every part of this performance is strictly true, I cannot help congratulating my brother-students on the great advantages we are likely to derive from these *big-bellied* professors, whose numbers have, in so short a time, been doubled, without any expence to the University.—" AND some of them of as high characters, as perhaps, ever filled those *chairs* in any University." Just now they were professors— then his Majesty endowed them——then they were filled with other professors—and now, at last, (strange metamorphosis!) they are turned into *chairs*. I remember, in one of the modern pantomimes, some grave justices of the peace are, by the artful turning

turning of the feats on which they fit, transformed into old women:—But this trick of converting the profeſſors of the Univerſity into *chairs*, is ſo much grander a piece of legerdemain, that Harlequin muſt yield the palm to the preſent Provoſt.

We next are told, that "premiums were formerly, and are now, giving to the divinity and greek *lectures*;———it is determined, at his deſire, to extend them to the hebrew, hiſtorical, oratory, and common law *lectures*." [*Ante, p.* 137.]

The late Dr. *Madden* deſerves to be always held in remembrance, for his admirable inſtitution of premiums for ſuch ſtudents, as ſhould appear to the ſeveral examiners the beſt ſcholars in their reſpective claſſes. But he little dreamed that ſo great an alteration ſhould be made in a few years after his death; that the *ſtudents* ſhould loſe this grand incentive to diligence; and that premiums, inſtead of being diſtributed among them, as formerly, ſhould be confined to the *lectures themſelves.* —Perhaps it may be ſaid, that this is an error of the preſs, and that we ought in this place to read *lecturers.*— but the depriving us of our premiums, and giving them to our *lecturers*, would be ſuch partiality and injuſtice, that I cannot, for my own part, think the Provoſt has ſo extravagant and unjuſt a ſcheme in contemplation.

"He

"He has increased and *fixed* the number of chapels *in a week*."—[*Same Account, &c. Page* 9.]

The college chapel I have always thought too small, and by no means sufficiently magnificent for the only university in Ireland. The addition of a number of chapels to it would certainly render it more commodious than it is at present, and be the means of accommodating a greater number of persons during the celebration of Divine Service, than the old building can now contain. But whether *one large* edifice would not be more superb, is, I think, worthy of consideration.——When I read this passage, it immediately struck me that these chapels must be small additional buildings, like those which, according to the accounts of travellers, are annexed to Roman Catholick churches, and dedicated to particular saints;—and when I came to the word *fixed*, it naturally brought to my mind the city of Venice, which, we are told, is built on a number of *floating* islands, that have been *fixed* and consolidated by art. But that the provost should have been able to execute so great a work in so short a time as *a week*, astonished me so much, that I immediately ran down into the court, when, lo! the old chapel appeared in its old place, and not a single new building near it.——I lifted up my eyes in amazement, and went back to my friend's chambers, suspecting that I had made some mistake: but I found the passage just as it is above quoted, and

and muſt leave the interpretation of it to ſome more able commentator.

I have now, I fear, tired my reader as well as myſelf; yet, I cannot omit the following *elegant* phraſes:

"The ſchoolmaſter of the ſchool in Kilkenny has "been *written to*." [*P.* 133.] "He has directed the "oratory profeſſor and his aſſiſtant, the tutors, the "morning lecturers, and the cenſor, to ſelect the "beſt exerciſes given in to them, and *to hand them* "*over to him, to ſee* which of them deſerve to be "diſtinguiſhed." [*P.* 134.] "Yet thoſe profeſſorſhips "have been all them *leſs uſeful*, and ſome of them "of *little* uſe." [*P.* 136.]

So that the degrees of compariſon muſt hereafter be changed in all Engliſh grammars, and run thus —*leſs—little—leaſt*.

"He has ordered that the rolls ſhould be called "but once, and that on the firſt morning only, *and* "*to be finiſhed* before eight o'clock." [*P.* 10.] "He "has alſo declared his intention of providing com- "mon rooms for the accommodation of the gentle- "men of the college; one for the fellows and gra- "duates, the other for the under-graduates, in the "manner of Oxford and Cambridge; and as thoſe "rooms will be ſupplied with newſpapers, tea, "coffee, &c. it is hoped *it* may be the means, by

"making

" making the college more agreeable to the stu-
" dents, of preventing them from going so very fre-
" quently into town. [*P.* 9.] That is, either the
rooms, the papers, the tea, or the coffee; for, by *it*,
any of these is clearly understood.

" This *(the Law)* lecture, which has been hi-
" therto of little or no use in this university, is now
" placed upon such a footing, as under the super-
" intendency of the provost who proposes to assist in
" the yearly examination, and sometimes to prelect
" *and in the hands of the present able professor,* † will
" make it a very great national benefit to this king-
" dom,"

The abilities of the present law-professor are
universally acknowledged—but, whether he is able
to sustain the present provost *in his hands* (as *Glum-dalclitch* used to exhibit *Gulliver)* for so long a time
as must necessarily be employed in delivering a *pre-lection*, may admit of some doubt.

Demosthenes is said to have transcribed the history
of *Thucydides* nine times. The learned writer of
this account seems to have been equally diligent in
studying and copying the *acta diurna* of an eminent
modern historian.——*Dr. Hurd* has proved the
marks of *imitation* to be so equivocal, that I shall
not

---

† The provost seems to have borrowed this idea from an
an ancient Medallion found at Herculaneum, of which we have
given a copy at the head of this number.

not presume to speak decisively on this subject; but
to me *the account* appears clearly to be written (to
use the language of painting) *con amore*, and in the
very best manner of a certain well-known and facetious Journalist *.

*These are some of the remarkable passages of this
work. If any thing has been interpolated, let the in-
terpolation be stated; if any thing that ought to have
been mentioned has been omitted, let the omission be
stated. Students may be amused, but, I hope, will not
be misled by such a model of composition as that which
has been now exhibited to them.*

STULTIFEX ACADEMICUS.

No. 28.   *Friday, January* 27, 1775.

Exemplar vitiis imitabile.   HOR.

TO THE PRINTER OF THE HIBERNIAN JOURNAL.

SIR,

AS this is the first time I have addressed you,
though you have written so many letters to
me, I hope you will afford a place in your paper
to a very few lines on a subject, which at present
seems to engage the attention of the publick; I mean
the

* Mr. George Faulkner.

the conduct and writings of a certain right honourable gem'man; each of which having been entirely misunderstood, I beg leave to set people right about them.

It has been very industriously given out that he solicited and accepted the provostship in order to step from thence to the chancery bench; but nothing, I am confident, was farther from his thoughts.——The truth is, it was merely by way of experiment, and for the encouragement of literature, that, like my *old* friend, *Berkley*, ‡ he thus *hung* himself up in the eye of the publick. But indeed the joke has been carried rather too far; and as the poor gem'man seems to be tired of his elevation, and to wish himself on the ground again, common humanity obliges me (though we are not on the most friendly terms) to lend him a hand, and to help to *cut him down*. This gem'man, every body knows, was always fond of pretty speeches, and has also a knack at composition. Now he could not but have observed, that the university in this kingdom, though it has sent out some very learned men, is very deficient in both these particulars, not having produced more than two or three authors in an age.——By *thrusting* himself, therefore, into a station, for which the whole tenour of his life and studies had rendered him eminently unqualified, he knew he should rouse the indignation of every student in the university; and he had not, I suppose, forgot what some *old* poet or other says—*facit in-*
dignatio.

‡ The bishop of Cloyne.

dignatio verſus.—It was *merely*, therefore, to *encourage compoſition*, that he climbed up to his preſent elevation; and all his violent proceedings, ſince he was inveſted with his preſent office, were clearly with the ſame view——and does he not appear as conſummate a politician in this, as in every other act of his life? Did any ſcheme ever ſucceed better? He has imped the wings of many promiſing young writers, and taught them to ſoar to heights that they never would otherwiſe have aſpired to.—Even me, he has made flowery—though, to own the truth, I never was very fond of flowers and fine ſpeeches——ſo that the railers againſt him are exceedingly miſtaken; for while they think they are degrading him, he is laughing in his ſleeve, and rejoices to find that he has, in a ſhort time, and in his own perſon, giving greater encouragement to compoſition than all the premiums that ever were diſtributed in the univerſity.

The writings of this gem'man have been as much miſunderſtood as his conduct. One *Dr. Lowth*, I am told, has written a very *clever* grammar on a new plan, illuſtrated by examples of what people ought to avoid.—The ingeniouſneſs of the idea ſtruck the provoſt; and he thought he could not by any method promote his favourite ſcheme ſo well, as by exhibiting in one view to the young gem'men under his care *ſtriking examples* of every illegitimate mode of expreſſion that the Engliſh language affords.—This is the true origin of his *Account of the regulations*

regulations made in Trinity College since his appointment to the office of provost.—Instead, therefore, of lessening his reputation, by enumerating the mistakes and inaccuracies of that *admirable* work, *Stultifex Academicus,* and the other gibers, who have criticised that performance, have in fact erected one more trophy to his fame.

Tho' I have not I must own, any great affection for him, yet at the same time I am so desirous that the *true character and designs* of this gem'man should be known and understood, that I shall add a few more instances of *premeditated* inaccuracy to those which have already been laid before the publick.

" This will for the future be prevented by a re-
" gulation proposed by the provost, and adopted
" by the board, obliging the batchelors to attend
" the lectures directed for that profession for which
" they have declared, and punishing them for not
" attending, or for negligence, by private admo-
" nishment for the offence of the first term, public
" admonishment for *the second,* and removal from
" the college *for the third."* [*Some Account, &c.* page 6.]

That is, for the second offence of the first time, and for the third offence of the same term—alas! poor Hillary! What unpardonable offence hast thou committed? However, this extraordinary severity is compensated by a suitable relaxation afterwards—
for

for from this paragraph we may fairly conclude, that during the *other three terms* a continued *jubilee* is to be kept.

" *The improvement* of the undergraduate courfe, and obliging the batchelors in their refpective *lines of ftudies* to attend the profeffors of thofe branches to which they are to *apply, will form as complete a fyftem* of education as any in Europe." [*Some Account*, &c. p. 8.]

This paffage is fufficiently illuftrated by Italicks.

" He has fhut up all accefs directly from the
" town to the college park, which had become a
" common walk, and frequently for company of
" the loweft and worft kind, *and was made a com-*
" *mon paffage.*" [*Some Account*, &c. p. 8.]

There is no one, I believe, who would not have been ftruck by the extraordinary manner in which the latter words printed in Italicks, are connected with the foregoing, if a fimilar arrangement had not occurred in the preceding paragraph———" The
" provoft has propofed and the board has agreed to
" the erecting new buildings, which will form a
" fquare, each fide of which will be about two
" hundred and twenty feet in length ; *and three*
" *fides of it will be new* ; this is to be begun imme-
" diately." Ibid.

Indeed

Indeed the provoſt cannot claim any *original* merit in thus tacking an *appendix* to a paragraph after it has been fairly cloſed; his facetious prototype having been long *admired* for a ſimilar arrangment.

" He has ordered that the roll ſhould be called " *but once*, and that on the firſt morning *only, and* " to be finiſhed before eight o'clock." [*Some Account*, &c. p. 10.]

So that on *the ſecond* morning the roll may with great propriety be called *twice*; whereby leſs time will be conſumed by this idle ceremony than formerly.

If the ſeveral paſſages that I have now cited were not written with the beſt intention and for the purpoſe of warning the young gem'man of the univerſity againſt writing inaccurate or inelegant Engliſh, I ſhould be extremely glad to be informed for what purpoſe they were intended.

OLD SLY-BOOTS.

No. 29,

No. 29.   *Monday, January* 30, 1775.

*Numquid nos agimus caufas? civilia jura,
Novimus? aut ullo ftrepitu fora veftra movemus?*
                                                   Juv.

MEMOIRS OF THE LIFE AND SURPRISING AD-
VENTURES OF MRS. COLLEGE.

MRS. COLLEGE was a comely lady, of a refpectable family, good reputation, and opulent circumftances. She had confiderable eftates; but the moft valuable and dignified of her poffeffions was an endowed free-fchool, which fhe managed by affiftant-mafters and ufhers, under the infpection of a principal appointed by the king, and held on condition of marrying the principal for the time being. This lady's firft hufband was *Frank Bluff*, † a fwaggering, tearing, curfing, fwearing, merry, witty, racketting, rakehelly, eating, drinking, laughing, fhrewd, fenfible, cunning fellow, who loved his friend, his bottle and his miftrefs; yet always had

an

† The late doctor F—— A———,

an eye to bufinefs, and mixed a proper portion of *utile* with his *dulce*:—With all his faults, Frank was good-natured and good-humoured — except when he was contradicted;—then, to be fure, he, would throw the tables and forms about the fchool room, and rap out an oath or two;—but fuch was the livelinefs of his wit, the open cordiality and endearing, communicative jollity of his manner, that every body liked him;—and his comrades would often fay, that " Frank Bluff was a comical dog—a damned honeft fellow."

When Mr. Bluff died, there were many candidates for the fchool, and (of courfe) fuitors to the widow. The good lady was not much afflicted at her lofs, as Frank had been too much a man of pleafure to make a tender hufband; fhe expreffed, however, a decent forrow; her weeds were becoming, and her behaviour exemplary, as the handfome and unexpected jointure which he left her demanded.——The widow had no objection to a fecond match; but the additional tenure by which fhe was to keep the fchool, as it precluded choice, diftreffed her: fhe feared his majefty and fhe might differ in their notions of a proper principal for the fchool, and fometimes refolved to give up all pretences to it, and retire, with the man of her choice, to content and a cottage; but her friends over-ruled fuch idle, romantick notions, and obliged her to accept the hand of Mr. *Jack Prance, attorney,* who was nominated principal of the fchool on account of his

fkill

skill in *fencing* and *horsemanship*, which recommended him to the notice of a *ministerial soldier*; especially as Mr. Prance promised to be as great a *disciplinarian* in the capacity of a schoolmaster, as his military *patron*, the *secretary*, was in that of an officer. The nuptials were solemnized in due form. Prance made an affecting speech on the occasion, in which he lamented his *poor abilities*, implored the *advice* of the assistant masters, and engaged to take care of the *health* and *morals* of the children, and gave a holiday to the boys, and a treat to the masters and ushers at the gridiron and three pigeons. Prance, who, as well as his predecessor, had a voice at the *parish vestry*, and was (like him) on the *commission of the peace*—was as assiduous in doing certain jobs at the vestry or sessions-house for *Sir Simon Stiffrump* the president, as that gentleman had been in performing such services for *Sir Brandy Bumper*, the late lord of the manor. The masters, ushers, and head boys of this school had a right to elect two monitors, who were entitled, for a certain term of years, to vote at the parish vestry. Now, in order to facilitate the aforesaid jobs, these gentlemen wished to secure the concurrence of the monitors; and this they proposed to effect by influencing the electors, and persuading (or compelling) them to choose persons recommended by their principal: their intrigues with the masters and scholars, to obtain this favourite aim, were a source of endless complaints, bickerings, heart-burnings, and discontents; and some acts of injustice, insolence, and

cruelty,

cruelty, to refractory individuals, (even in Bluff's time) almost drove the boys to a barring-out; and it required all his acuteness and good sense to weather the storm.

The election of new monitors approached.—— Prance attached himself to doctor *Dilemma*, a man of some learning and abilities—of much vanity and presumption—of *inordinate ambition* and *indecent resentment*. This gentleman, by new arguments of his own, endeavoured to lead boys to a right sense of implicit obedience, and extort a promise of voting, *hap-hazard*, for whatever candidates their principal should offer to their acceptance: but the unlucky rogues laughed at the poor gentleman, and said, " they had no notion of *buying a pig in a poke*, or making their election a game at *blindman's buff*." Our little pedagogue was exceedingly mortified at this insolent disobedience, (as he called it.) Some violent, some wicked, and very many foolish and laughable measures were pursued. The boys were enraged—the masters and ushers murmured—the good were afflicted, and the mischievous diverted. Lampoons and pasquinades were stuck up on the walls of the school-room, and the press teemed with ballads;—some of the boys were whipt for singing them, but to no purpose;— a new ballad was made on that, and the boys roared it louder than any of the old ones.

Jack, conscious of his abilities, convened the masters and scholars, in hopes of setting all to rights by

by an *oration*; and accordingly prepared to mount a table for that purpose, when doctor *Pompoſo* exclaimed, ' In the name of God, Mr. Principal, ' what are you about?—It might well be deemed ' *virulent* in me to ſuffer you to expoſe your feet, ſo ' lately reclaimed from the dominion of the gout, ' to a *conflict* with the hard table;—let me ſerve you ' for a ſuggeſtum—my ſhoulders will be ſoft and ' warm to them—and, I vow to the Lord! there ' will not be the ſmalleſt danger of my *ſuccumbing* ' under your auſpicious weight.' Doctor Pompoſo having a tolerable broad back, ſtooped, and ſupporting his hands with his own volumes of *the hiſtory of Quagmire*, and *life of Philip Filch*, formed a commodious *ſuggeſtum*; on which Jack Prance mounted, and delivered,——

The ORATION *of* JACK PRANCE, *as it was pronounced from the back of* DOCTOR POMPOSO.

" I am happy to addreſs myſelf on a queſtion as ' *important* as any that was ever agitated in this, or ' any aſſembly, to *ſuperior* men, gentlemen of your ' diſtinguiſhed candour, exalted abilities, profound " learning, attention to the duties of your ſtation, " integrity, and morals—Men who unite the virtues " of the cloyſter and court—accurate diſciplinari-
" ans—accompliſhed courtiers. I am the creature " of your wiſdoms. I ſpeak not to give, but to " elicit information; and I hope (without vanity I " ſay it) to convince you all, *as clear as the ſun at* " *noon-day*, that, like a parcel of droning, lazy,
" weak,

"weak, stupid, sottish, knavish dotards, you scan-
"dalously, maliciously, falsely, and treacherously
"deserted, slighted, and betrayed the interests of the
"school. I have the highest deference to your opi-
"nion, and the greatest esteem for you, gentlemen;
"and assure you, with the most unfeigned respect,
"that you are a set of good-for-nothing *blockheads*.
"Your Park, gentlemen!—every tree, every blade
"of grass in it cries shame!—Though no lapse es-
"capes reprehension, or eludes notice, you suffered
"it to be crowded every Sunday with a resort of
"disorderly company—*barbers' boys*, pick-pockets,
"women of the town, mantua-makers, milliners,
"sempstresses, and chamber-maids—to the ruin of
"the health and morals of young minds, open to
"every impression, yielding to every infusion.
"This evil, this fatal canker, was left for me to
"remedy, and I have remedied it.

"Though you are a set of people (I assert it
"*confidentially*) as respectable, all and every of you,
"as any in Europe;—yet there are some of you
"vagabonds, unfit to discharge the duties and fill
"the employment of dean. I have looked out the
"honestest man, and best *disciplinarian*, among you,
"to be junior dean, and have already reaped many
"advantages from his advice and assistance, and
"hope for more. The *natives* were formerly very
"absurdly and idly disposed, according to seniority;
"they are now to be given on a new plan, propos-
"ed by the *dean*, approved by me.——1st, accord-
"ing

" ing to their voting *properly*—2dly, according to
" my *hopes* of their voting *properly*—3dly, accord-
" ing to the recommendations of my friend, doctor
" *Dilemma*—4thly, according to the *connection* be-
" tween their parents and me—and 5thly, (and
" *lastly)* according to the merits, political and con-
" vivial of their respective masters. I am not actu-
" ated in what I say by *ambition* or *interest*—by
" little schemes of *electioneering policy*.

" To convince you of my care of the public
" welfare, and the purity of my intentions, you
" need not be told, that I intend to build a new
" square, (to be called *Harcourt Square)* 700 feet in
" length, and 400 in breadth, (as soon as we can
" persuade parliament to give us money for that
" purpose) with an equestrian statue of our glorious
" foundress in the middle, which will be a great
" ornament to this learned seminary. Three dol-
" phins of lead shall spout up water, which shall
" fall again into an octagonal square bason of white
" marble. The boys in the school are 555;—those
" that reside are 255;—the remaining 300 lived in
" beer-cellars, tap-rooms, b———y-houses, taverns,
" coffee-houses, billiard-tables, tennis-courts, and
" other highly improper places: I took them all
" away from thence, in spite of the authority of
" their fathers, mothers, uncles, aunts, and guar-
" dians, as my friend, *Mendax*, here under my
" feet, can *testify* ;—and for their reception, until
" the erection of the court aforesaid, I have pro-
" vided

"vided *castles* in the *air*;—the rest, who think
"that too *cold* a lodging, I shall take the liberty of
"billetting, four on a master, two on an usher.
"The calling the roll but once during every exa-
"mination, is a most useful regulation, on which I
"value myself extremely, as it gives an indulgent
"tutor an opportunity of obliging his own pupils
"in his division, by allowing them to absent them-
"selves after the first morning, and giving them
"credit, and handing over their judgments to the
"senior lecturer, as answerers of a whole examina-
"tion.

"All your lectures have been of very little use,
"most of them are of none, particularly divinity
"and mathematics, (which I propose to superintend
"myself) though it is well known they are filled
"with gentlemen as able as any in this or any uni-
"versity; men of brilliancy of genius, equal to
"their depth of learning, ever attentive to the du-
"ties of their station, clear to elucidate, patient to
"instruct; yet *those chairs* have been noted all over
"Europe for their shameful inattention to their of-
"fice, for the little benefit derived from them to
"those *who do not attend them*; this will appear as
"clear as the midnight sun, when I inform you
"that there are two classes of attendants on lec-
"tures; *careless attendants* and non-attendants.
"The abilities of doctor Pomposo, under my feet
"here, are known, confessed. He is a *superior*
"man, his example, his learning, his eloquence
"(for

"(for he is a very *eloquent man*) his *pleasing man-
"*ners*, his affiduity, and attention, render *this chair
"* the moſt reſpectable perhaps in the known world,
"* nay in Europe.* But the doctor is very ill qualified
" for the duties of his employment, and his affiſtant
" ſtill worſe, which I propoſe to remedy by teach-
" ing them both to read myſelf, and attending as
" their aſſeſſor; oratory lecture has been very much
" neglected, owing to the non-attendance or care-
" leſs attendance of gentlemen to which, as well as
" that of other lectures, I offer this remedy : to
" neglect of the firſt term, we will give a caution ;
" on that of the ſecond we will beſtow an admoniſh-
" ment ; and the conſequence of the third neglect
" ſhall be removing from the ſchool; and this may
" conduce mightily to the peace and good order of
" the ſchool, by giving me an opportunity of re-
" moving refractory ſpirits who *let* and hinder the
" principal in his ſchemes; clap drags on the
" wheels of government, and ſpill the oil intended
" to greaſe the wheels and ſprings of that vaſt and
" complicated machine. For lectures ſhall be mul-
" tiplied, that it will be morally impoſſible to at-
" tend all, and we will eaſily remove the factious
" and ſeditious for non-attendance. I intend to
" give premiums *to* all ſorts of *lectures*; *they are a
"* deſerving ſet of people* and ſhould be encouraged ;
" beſides, I can by this means multiply the incen-
" tives to pliability, and convey little *douceurs* to
" gentlemen that *cultivate* me *properly* ; under the
" name of Hebrew, Greek, Divinity, Hiſtory, Ora-

" tory

"tory Premiums. I am not a little proud of this
"hit: the *attendants* on some of these lecture
"have long been encouraged by premiums; I was
"the first who invented giving them to *lectures*
"*themselves*. Discipline is the nerve and sinew of
"government; to promote it, I propose (with your
"approbation) to erect a ducking chair, and dig a
"deep bason of water for that machine to play in.
"This will also conduce to the health of the boys,
"by giving them an opportunity of bathing,
"swimming, and amusing themselves with dog and
"duck, and such literary and elegant recreations.
"I propose to build a fencing school, fifty foot by
"thirty in the clear; and in a field contiguous,
"buts shall be erected to fire pistols at. This pro-
"fessorship (though I am conscious of my own ina-
"bility) I will, with your permission, take on my-
"self, happy if my poor endeavours shall prove ser-
"viceable to the place of my early education. I
"mean to give a lecture every day; every gentle-
"man will be obliged to attend, as I have felt the
"necessity to every one of a knowledge of the *wea-*
"*pons*. Premiums of silver-hilted *swords* will be
"given to this lecture.—Law lecture, now worth-
"less and contemptible, I propose in a short time
"to make exceeding good, by giving the professor
"advice, assistance, and instructions; every boy in
"the school shall attend, as a knowledge of the law
"of the land is necessary to every one. Twice a
"week he shall lecture them in those books which
"they *do*, and once a year examine in those which
"they

"they do *not* read; premiums shall be given to their answering out of both. I myself will attend, inspect, and prelect occasionally. This will be a vast saving of money to the kingdom; templars need only be three months in the year in England to save the terms; the constant sailing to and fro will be excellent for their health, and take up time which else might be wasted in debauchery; and I pledge myself, by my connections at the other side the water, and my interest with the admiralty office, to ensure a fair wind from Parkgate to Dublin, or from Dublin to Parkgate, on producing a certificate from law lecture.

"For those that are apt to be sea-sick, or wish a shorter passage, I have prevailed with an ingenious artist, to run a flying machine, drawn by dragons from Dublin to Pargate in half an hour, and propose to *resign* 200*l. per annum out of my own salary*, for maintaining him and his dragons and repairing his chariot —Of my intended riding-house I have spoke so often, and so fully, I have nothing to add, but that I am pleased with this opportunity of providing for an ingenious friend, whom I value for his *wit, liberal sentiments*, and *eloignement* from vulgar *prejudices*. Galen, Paracelsus, Diodorus, Siculus, Varro, Pliny and all the other medical writers are loud in praise of ligneous equitation; now I intend to present each of you, gentlemen, with an easy

"*see-saw-pad*; an useful amusement for a sedentary
"man, both for pleasure and health, would be
"a ride on one of these, of a rainy day: besides
"a happy union of the Roman lyrick's *utile* and
"*dulce*, by presenting health and instilling the
"rudiments of the manege; and I will attend
"and give my best instructions with an eye to
"mounting the horse with grace and agility, and
"sitting him with ease and firmness. I intend
"to provide a large field for athletick exercises,
"foot-ball, goff, cricket, and hurling; (which my
"*son tells me* are practised at *Eton*.) I propose to
"erect a tennis-court, a ball-yard and a skittle
"ground, which I hope will endear me to the
"younger members. I propose to have a professor
"of dancing; (Mr. *Michel* that teaches my Chil-
"dren; a man of signal abilities) to give dan-
"cing premiums and oblige all the boys to at-
"tend dancing lectures. I will build an univer-
"sity ball-room for balls once a week, under my
"own inspection, and that of the two deans.
"Of my professors of modern tongues, French,
"Italian, Dutch, German, Solecismic and Otaheite,
"you have been often told. All these amusements
"will endear the school to the boys, and prevent
"their mitching in quest of amusement, especially
"when my theatre is built, and we act publick-
"private *plays*. I imagine there then will be no
"desire to strole into town to the play houses. I
"also mean to set up a common room, with tea,
"coffee, pipes and news papers; and with a view
"to

"to make this entertainment elegant and inftruc-
"tive, I wrote my *Moderators* to raife the ftyle
"of news-paper effays. As many of our ftudents
"may be called hereafter to feats in the higher or
"lower houfe of parliament, this will be a moft
"important inftitution; they will go from us,
"not unacquainted with the interefts, not carelefs
"of the conftitution of their country, by imbibing
"political rudiments with their coffee, and de-
"bating queftions of national import at their
"meetings; and for the furthering thofe purpofes,
"I pledge myfelf to write once a week in fome of
"the publick papers, and that I may promote fo
"great a national benefit, I will attend myfelf,
"and prelect in politicks. I intend to give compo-
"fition-premiums; I am fure you will allow my
"plan for that purpofe as ingenious, as it is novel.
"On the Irifh rebellion, Gunpowder plot, King
"Charle's reftoration, the King's birth day, de-
"clamations have been patched up, or copied
"traditionally from archetypal compilations.
"I intend to give premiums,——firft, to all the
"ancient hereditary fpeeches; and when they
"are provided for, all the graduates that pleafe
"may fend in fpeeches; the beft to be felected,
"fpoken and get premiums. This, I prefume,
"will be an encouragement to compofition, as
"great as ever was attempted in *any* univerfity
"in *any* kingdom. Firft the *novelty* of the fub-
"ject will call forth abilities, and give an eclat
"and luftre to the compofition. Secondly, the
"fubjects

"subjects are the finest that ever agitated on
"oratory genius, in this or any kingdom. These
"different subjects will call forth the different styles
"and colours of eloquence. The rebellion and
"the plot will exercise the invective and the pathe-
"tic; the restoration and the birth-day, the
"diffusive, the magnificent and the panegyrical;
"so here we shall have all the provinces of the
"compleat orator; as enumerated by *Tully* in
"his *tract de oratore*, which I intend to make all
"our young gentlemen read, especially panegyrick,
"the most useful to the orator and indeed to every
"body, as my Lord Chesterfield, in his invalua-
"ble, and never enough to be studied letters tells
"us. I propose, to give young gentlemen a proper
"notion of the *graces*, to introduce Lord Chester-
"field into our course; he may be read together
"with Xenophon's oeconomics, and will make
"a fine system of domestick management. Xeno-
"phon's oeconomics is my favourite volume; my
"houshold is regulated by his plan.

"Lord Chesterfield, in his letters, an inesti-
"mable volume that deserves to be wrote in
"letters of gold, has shewn the importance of
"the *graces*: those attainments are indeed im-
"portant; they are consequential, they are all
"in all. To the *graces* I must attribute my rise
"in the world; do but mind my graceful parade
"when I come into a public place, and you will
"own this. They will now be within our pale;
                                          "every

" every student may reach them. Formerly (and
" I beheld it with regret) our youth were compel-
" led to range through Europe, to gather those
" polite endowments, which (if I may use the
" similitude) like a nosegay in the breast of a beauty,
" adorn and finish the man of sense. Now they
" bloom like domestick roses in our own garden,
" every youth that pleases may pluck them.

" My schemes extend still further: the profes-
" sor of musick has been hitherto a mere sinecure.
" I propose, with your assistance, to make it an
" active, an useful office, by appointing an able
" assistant with a competent salary. Lectures
" shall be read twice, Solos performed once a week,
" with a musick prelection and grand concert once
" a month. Thus the taste for *Italian Musick*, for
" which gentlemen were obliged to travel, may
" be had for a small expence of time and money
" at home. These attainments may be a means
" of bringing into the world gentlemen of deep
" learning but shallow finances, who choose to
" embark as private tutors; by enabling them to
" act as masters of languages, to teach the young
" gentlemen the *Manege*, and skill in their *weapons*;
" the young *ladies* of the family to *dance* and play
" the *Guitar* and *Harpsichord*. This, gentlemen,
" is a great, it is a national advantage; it will,
" if I may use the metaphor, lay the axe to the
" root of the expensive folly of visiting foreign
" countries. The consequence will be, the future
" and."

"and superior accomplishments of the next ge-
"neration; the present saving of money to the
"kingdom, and the merit of this I must (it is
"a virtuous vanity) take to myself. Yes, I own
"I look forward with transport to the completion
"of my schemes, and consider myself as a na-
"tional benefactor. To complete all these my
"schemes, I propose to encrease the *College* reve-
"nue, by refusing fines, letting the leases run
"out, and setting the lands to the younger
"bradches of my family. The father of many
"children is a benefactor to the publick; I look
"with pleasure on my numerous progeny, as
"it gives a hope of supplying you out of my
"own family with *fellows*, who will read *Thu-*
"*cydides* and be fine disciplinarians; and with
"punctual tenants. This want of the usual fines
"may be a present distress, but no gentleman will
"yield to, or be influenced by such reflections,
"when your present distress and diminution of
"income leads to the future opulence of your
"successors, and a comfortable provision for my
"younger children. I assure you, little Abraham,
"my son, construes Demosthenes and Aristotle's
"poeticks at sight already; I hope and trust he
"will one day be your tenant. The policy that
"bounds all in the narrow centre of self, is base,
"is low; you to use Mr. Pope's sublime *allusion*,
"will expand it till it embraces all human kind.
"I have wrote down these things in a small tract
"which the junior boys shall read with their logick,
"and

" and my learned and elegant friend's doctrine of
" dilemmas. I have sent it to Oxford and Cam-
" bridge, that those learned seminaries may see a
" younger sister setting them an example of new arts
" and attainments, dignified as they are important.
" All my cares, my labours, sacrificing my reputa-
" tion, my health, my time and ease, calling boards
" and making speeches, writing in newspapers and
" enditing pamphlets, have been for the publick
" good; let public justice be their reward."—Here
Jack descended from the rostrum, and was called on
an important occasion; what that was will appear
in the next chapter.

No. 30. *Wednesday, February 1, 1775.*

Dat veniam corvis; vexat censura columbas.   JUV.

TO THE PRINTER OF THE HIBERNIAN JOURNAL.

SIR,

I Appeal to your candour and that of the publick, in defence of our injured and calumniated Provost. His own pen (I am conscious) is amply sufficient for the task; yet, if my toils can save to the publick even a few of the valuable moments, which should all be sacred to the accomplishment of the many great and extensive plans which our learned head has projected for the *improvement* of the college, I shall not have laboured in vain; be that as it may, this weak display of good-will must be serviceable to me, as it will be not unpleasing to the provost; *forsan & hæc olim meminisse juvabit*. His gratitude to real friends has been shewn in obtaining a snug benefice for Doctor Dilemma, whose politeness and politics will one day obtain and adorn a mitre. Your facetious correspondent, *Stultifex*, has called our provost whose abilities, it must be owned, are of the very first *magnitude*) a *man-mountain*; if he is a *man-mountain*, there are not wanting virulent *pigmies*, malignant *little* medlers, who divert themselves and the publick by running their *tiny lances* up his nostrils. Dear sir, consider the consequences of such envenomed publications. With the attention to fame, and nice sensibility inseparable from refined spirits, the Provost peruses the public papers, and agonizes when they contain invective. I can assure you (from the best authority) *that* wicked Stultifex cost the poor gentleman a fit of the gout, confined him to his bed, and robbed the college of the advantages which it would have derived from a conference on oratory and composition, which was appointed for last Wednesday, but unhappily prorogued by Stultifex. The chain of reasonings in his laborious and eloquent little *pamphlet*, has been misrepresented and called an argument *non ad idem*. What strange confusion of ideas? or, rather, what *affected* dulness could misapprehend the drift of that performance?

performance?—Facts, that is, *promises*—were collected (but his promises are facts) and from a state of them every reasonable man might see, whether the college had or had *not* received any benefit or improvement since the appointment of the present provost. Men might see what had been done (that is, *promised*) in six months, and judge what might be *performed* in years to come; and surely every grateful, every wise man would readily draw the conclusion;——if this man has laboured so abundantly (in *idea*) for the good of the college, and *promises* to labour yet more; indulge him (in gratitude for the past, in hope of the future) indulge him in returning the men of his choice, ' This, ' gentlemen (he would say) the first request I ever ' made you, is a mere trifle; what is it to you, ' Doctor, or you, or you—who sits in the senate ' house? Studious men should not leave their books ' to meddle with politicks; and therefore govern-- ' ment wisely sets political men over them, who will ' think for them all, and furnish them with political ' opinions ready made to their hands.'—*Stultifex* has enlarged on inaccuracies of style (as he is pleased to think them) with malicious triumph; but I would ask him,—whence are the rules of the epopee derived, but from the poems of Homer? Rules are ever collected from the practice of the successful; and exalted spirits are born to create rules, not to obey them. Consider what reputation for eloquence our provost has acquired, and what wealth he has amassed by his pleadings; and deny if you

dare,

dare, his being entitled to new-model our language, and establish a dialect of *his own*, by introducing *Prancerisms*, and coining new modes of diction, or even *degrees* of *comparison*. There is one gross mistake, which shews the ignorance and dulness of this would-be critic; I mean his representing the provost, as erecting a weekly number of chapels. What head but his own would have conceived the possibility of such a thing?—Were such a number of chapels to be weekly raised, where would the provost find room for the pious labours of his hands? First, they would block up our courts, then overspread the park, and at last fill up the streets and lanes of the city, and leave no room for other necessary buildings; so that perhaps we should see the college *chapels* presented as a *nuisance* by the Dublin *Grand Jury*, or an act of parliament passed to prevent the unlawful encrease of chapels. He must be a *devil* of a provost indeed, who raises chapels Pandæmonium-like with the swiftness of an exhalation.—The appearance of our chapel lighted up for evening service in winter, ever recalled to my mind the lines of Milton:

——————— From the arched roof
Pendent, by subtle magic, many a row
Of starry lamps, with blazing cressets fed
Of Naptha and Asphaltus, yielded light
As from a sky.———

Perhaps

Perhaps the smart observer took his hint from thence, and meant to insinuate a similitude between our governor and the diabolical builder of Pandæmonium. *Stultifex* (who ought rather to be called *Stultus*) says he is a student of our college:—Now, gentlemen, if I can convict him of falsehood in this assertion, the publick will know in what degree of credit to hold his testimony.——What! a student of our college, and not know the meaning of terms with which every Irishman is acquainted;—chapels and tardies are terms, which (though barbarous and insignificant to strangers) serve college people well enough for communication, which (as Mr. Locke observes) is the great end of language;—they are among the terms of art, of which every trade or mystery hath a set peculiar to itself.—The provost's use of them, far from being a reproach to him, I think reflects the highest honour on him, as it shews such an attention to the duties of his station, that he has made himself master of all the *cant* words that are current in the college, and uses them as pertinently as if he had been provost from his cradle;—and I assure you, gentlemen, the acquisition of this knowledge has cost him many a weary hour, and encroached many a time on the business of the Four-courts. It is hardly credible with what indefatigable assiduity this injured gentleman has laboured to qualify himself for his present employment;—he has toiled like a horse, with the assistance of Dr. Forsayeth, (who has a distinguished character as a *disciplinarian*) to define the

magnitude

magnitude and ascertain the number of chapels, to search into the causes and remedies of tardies, and explore the fundamental principles and practice of night rolls. Permit me now, gentlemen, no lay before you a few of the principal regulations for which the college is indebted to the present provost for this purpose.

I shall observe first, how all offences have been *investigated* with the strictest attention, insomuch, that by the industry and ingenuity of our *worthy provost*, many new crimes have been discovered, which are not so much as *named* in the statutes, and which *no one* suspected to be offences, until his *useful labours* pointed out the discovery. 2dly, the provost has *proposed*, and the board has *agreed* to the erecting of *new* buildings, which will form a *square*, each side of which will be about 220 feet in length, and *three* sides of it will be *new*; and this is to be begun immediately. The fourth side will not be *new*, but *old* buildings built quite *new*, on the very best plan of ruins now extant. The art of building *ruins* has been brought to a high pitch in these days. Among other monuments of his genius, the provost proposes to give an instance of his taste for that style of architecture, by making one side of his intended *new* square a venerable *old* ruin. He, as a practised *improver*, well knows what a delightful termination to a *visto* is afforded by a ruin. Perhaps in the *field* which is to be provided for the *exercises* of the youth, when it can be

be done with *convenience*, he may plant a dark walk, which will end in his *ruin*. Oxford and Cambridge are full of Gothick spires, chapels, cathedrals, and other ancient edifices, which, by filling the mind with a religious awe, and disposing it to serious meditation, contribute not a little to the superior learning and poetical genius, which it must be owned are displayed at these universities. Something of the same kind is wanting to give our university that gloomy solemnity so proper in a seat of learning, and so well fitted to excite philosophical musings; and this *great* defect will soon be remedied by our *intended ruin*. 3dly, Nothing is so commendable in the head of a learned seminary as an attention to the duties of religion. The provost, with grief observed, that the number of chapels in a week was shamefully diminished;—and, to restore a commendable spirit of devotion in the university, the provost has proposed, and the board at his instance agreed, that the great bell shall be tolled for early prayers: the little bell was formerly employed on this service, and found insufficient, such was the drowsiness of the young gentlemen. It is now hoped that many whom neither a spirit of devotion, nor the clamours of their college women, can summon from their beds, may be roused to their duty by the thunders of the *great* bell;—— and lest these good intentions should be defeated by the carelessness and laziness of the college domestics, the provost (whose *eye*, like the *sun*, is every where) constantly attends in *person* to *see* the great
bell

bell tolled, and often assists in tolling it with his *own hands*. An unlucky accident happened lately at one of these morning exercises:---Our poor provost's leg was caught in the loop of the bell-rope; and he was now borne aloft to the cieling———then plunged down and dashed against the floor———insomuch, that if it had not been for the solidity of his head, or for a warm red night-cap which he wore, his brains must inevitably have been dashed out. 4thly, To complete his scheme for the encouragement of religion, the provost has devised a new expedient---which is to give *premiums* to *six o'clock* chapels, which will be an effectual means of encouraging (as he says) those diligent youths. These, gentlemen, are facts. Malevolent writers have torn a respectable character to pieces: be it my part to reunite the mangled limbs.

MARTINUS SCHOLASTICUS.

No. 31.   *Friday, Febuary 3, 1775.*

Ἱππαρχον κρεμασας μαστιγωσον.
                            PLUT. in ANT.

TO HIPPARCHUS.

†IF, in the prefent elevation of military fame (doubly dear from novelty) the voice of your *friend* can reach you, receive the congratulations of *Charidemus*, on the encreafe of your renown, and the fafety of your perfon: he as little hoped an addition to the former, as a hazard of the latter; but it is the ftudy of the generous *Hipparchus*, to gratify all his friends, who love to rail or to laugh, with fubjects beyond the meafure of their wifhes, and furprife them daily with fomething which ftartles belief, and fhames invention. You poffefs O Hipparchus! that noble boldnefs and promptitude of corruption, which rufh on through the clamours and curfes of men without hefitation or fear; and perpetually make the laft crime a ftep to a greater; that happy alertnefs of folly for ever buft-
                                            ling

† This paper appeared foon after the provoft had fought with William Doyle, Efq;

ling to display itself; and that noble enterprize of indiscretion for ever in quest of some undiscovered region of absurdity. Men void of principle and veracity are too apt to imagine that this want renders them consummate politicians;—you have *felt* that they fatally deceive themselves; perfidy and falshood, with prudence and temper, are powerful; you have *felt* that without them they are weak and unmanageable instruments—Had a comick writer invented such a series of transactions as your's, and described such a *ridiculous despotism, burlesque pomp,* and *beggarly parade* of learning and abilities, we should have condemned the pleasantry as inordinate, the delineation as overcharged. Had the satirical traveller made a governor of the literary state in Lagado, a projector of gaudy days, an erector of riding-houses; had he given him orations on any thing or nothing, solemnly read from notes deliberately written and publications of anonymous sophistry in answer to anonymous charges; had he introduced him summoning his council, and when they were supposed busy in settling some weighty point of learning or morals, setting them to construe the asterisks and fill up the blanks of the morning scribbler, to contrive or refute newspaper invectives, and then (to compleat the ridicule) to censure the readers of them; had he conducted this man (of whom it was said—he had one of the peaceful virtues, he was patient of injuries—a patience the more meritorious from his *vindictive nature,)* to a
field

field of battle in his *old age*, and killed in single combat; we should have condemned the humour as forced, the character as unnatural; and rejoiced in the *conclusion* of the tale.——You are a benefactor to the stage; you have added one to the stock of comick characters. Your kindness to the *satirist* is not less signal; you know what pleasure he receives, when the object of his invective feels the blow: you do not merely feel, you *agonize* under the touch; your conduct invites the attack, and your trembling sensibility assures his aim. To compleat your kindness, it is not an amiable pity-moving sensibility, that might awaken remorse in him that wounds it, or fix on him the charge of cruelty; it is the *sensibility* of *snails* and *toads* that emit (in *impotence* of *spite*) *frothy filth* or *venom*, while they shrink from the wound. Nothing can give more pleasure to the virtuous, than guilt, by ridiculous sensibility, rendered its own scourge; except it be a corrupt man and his wicked instruments, defeating pernicious schemes by their own folly; while dissimulation becomes sincerity; falshood, by its veracity uniformity, and the wheels within wheels of an oppressive *tyranny* take fire through the *rashness* of the movers.—It seems that the days of fascination have not yet ceased, and that some inchanter, leagued with the enemy of mankind commands his dæmon to hover round the head of Hipparchus, and influence his actions. Hence novelty has chaced novelty, proposed, dignified, declaimed on, assented to, and abandoned; and folly has tricked her cap with a

daily

daily project, scarcely worn, and given to the wind.
Yet, accustomed as they are to this magnificent exhibition of grand absurdity, your subjects were astonished (much as they well might expect from your talents) at a late *publication*, and a later *combat*. Your enemies taxed you with want of literary *abilities*; men who had never heard your *oratory*, and only knew it by *its fruits*, in your *aggrandizement*, might well have doubted the truth of this charge. You have politely proved its justice, and published a test of your abilities, such as your bitterest enemy would have dictated. In a late *tract* on *education*, confusion of ideas, ignorance of grammar, blunders, *barbarisms*, and vulgarities, are accumulated with such skill, that the composition is beneath an *advertising mechanick*; and did not the resemblance to your usual style of oratory appear too plainly, might be thought a mean attempt to disgrace you by imputed nonsense.——By dispersing this performance, however, with your *own hands*, you have prevented any doubt of its authenticity. Your insinuations to the prejudice of your predecessor—your endeavours to wound the memory of the dead—your pompous display of the wonders of *six months*—your injurious reflections on the state you govern—your representing it as sunk in sloth, depraved by luxury, ignorant of arts, void of discipline, and careless of religion—your modest comparisons between yourself and your predecessors on the throne, (comparisons which the public would have made of itself, too soon for your honour)—your libellous,

base,

base, and false imputations on the members of your council and the public rhetors, conveyed under fawning compliment and fulsome civility, which shew at once cowardice and malice, the desire and fear to wound—all these may determine the qualities of your heart. The stab aimed at the expounder of the laws is peculiarly envenomed. You inform the world, that his labours were hitherto *useless*; you promise to assist and instruct him in his department. Every man acquainted with our courts of justice knows what must be the understanding and legal knowledge that could really be indebted to your instructions. Your publishing a libel (that must rouse the most unfeeling to resentment, the most indolent to opposition) on your council—on men whom you wish to *attach* to your government, and render *subservient* to your measures, is consistent with your characteristick petulance, with the sickly peevishness of conscious infamy, with your ungentlemanly, indecent insolence, and outrageous, wanton insults on some of your most respectable subjects; and may determine your character as a politician. Your plans (the darling conceptions of your vanity) had been treated with contempt, and called the reveries of ignorance bewildered by power. Men might have suspected that the charge was groundless, or exaggerated. You have submitted schemes, that will astonish, provoke, and divert, to the publick; and men may judge for themselves.

They

They find, however, one subject for praise in these sallies of absurdity, that they are imperfect and abortive; they lie like the crude, unformed crawling reptiles, hatched in the mud of Nile; and not all the rays of oratorial sun-shine shall ripen them into *snakes* and *adders*. One step your friends and enemies wished to spare you—the sending a libel on your state and your subjects to *Thebes* and *Corinth*, as if one empire could not afford contempt enough for ravings, which even phrenzy would disclaim. Both your enemies and friends wished to hide your follies within your own kingdom, lest they should become publicly ridiculous, and find a share of contempt, reflected to them from the absurdities of their prince. The good, content with a vain opposition, blushed at, and wished to conceal their unhappy situation. The indolent and timid desired to bury measures, in which they concurred, in eternal silence. The adviser who planned, and the instrument who supported base or ridiculous measures, hoped to veil their depravity from the publick, and sink into oblivion with the tyranny they aided:—They may *thank* the pen of *Hipparchus* for a share in his *immortality of dishonour*. Must we attribute a late transaction to a return of the fondness you once shewed for the military profession, to the love of absurdity, or to a settled plan for ruining the city you govern?—It is a new thing under the Sun, to see the head of a learned city, a guardian of morals, a man appointed to restrain licentious youth, and

" recall

recall the eager paffions from outrage, againſt the laws of man or God—openly defying the laws of his country, which his profeffion peculiarly calls on him to maintain, and committing a crime which he is bound, by his office and his oath, to prevent. You have enlarged on the bleffings of your reign, the negligence of your predeceffors, the incapacity of your counfellors, the want of *difcipline* in your dominions ;—you furely meant *military*— a late tranfaction is fubverfive of all other. The laws of your ſtate are fo full and expreſs againſt quarrels and fanguinary juſtifications, that they do not permit your fubjects even to wear arms *. We are now more than ever convinced of the wifdom of the tradition, that the fovereign of this country ought to be a prieſt. Can the magiſtrate, with decency, puniſh the fubject for the very crime of which the fovereign has been guilty. The man who thought a trifling amufement demanded all the thunders of his invective—who ſtudied the laws fo diligently, noted down their purport in his clofet—and, in his zeal for morality, and the intereſts of religion, read his manufcript to his aſſembled fubjects, pompouſly referred them to the volume at large, dared to infinuate a charge of perjury, and, with a queſtion of accuſation, aſked
them

---

* We find a fimilar claufe, in a modern code : Statuimus & ordinamus ut nullus prædictorum Armis, &c. in collegio aut in urbe utatur.—In the fame code, Homicidium voluntarium, is numbered among the majora Crimina.

them if they remembered their oath, ‡ this man is found in a field of combat, in open defiance of our laws, and of the oath † by which he was bound to maintain them.——We shall be told of the customs of the world, and the difficulties of your situation. Duelling is a fatal remedy for the defects of law and police; sometimes necessary, never laudable. This ferocious practice is a supplement to the laws, and restrains men from transgression, by the fear of consequences; while the brutal, the perfidious, and the dissolute are awed into innocence; and by the prompt vengeance it inflicts, the domestick virtues, to whose preservation the laws could not extend, the decencies, the confidences, the respectable forbearances, and salutary restraints of life, are enforced. As the remedy is violent, it should not be applied, except where the laws have failed to provide redress, and the injured person would become infamous, lose his rank in life, intercourse with his fellow-citizens, happiness, and perhaps means of existence; where,

in

---

‡ In the same code we find a law against card playing which was originally intended to prevent *gaming*, but has lately been rigorously enforced, in order to deprive the fellows and scholars of the college of an *innocent* amusement, and to encourage *drinking*.

† There is a parallel passage in an oath recited in the same Code: Statuta hujus Collegii pro *virili mea* in omnibus servaturum iisque omnibus quæ ex eorum Præscripto gerentur meum Assensum accommodaturum, omnesque & singulos, &c. ex iisdem legibus & Statutis siue ullius Generis aut Conditionis, aut Personarum Respectu, gratia aut Odio recturum—*even a Son.*

in short, from the greatness of the offence, the necessity of punishing, and the silence of the legislator, the man returns to a state of nature in that instance. You had none of these reasons to justify your conduct; and the man is highly criminal in the sight of his country and his God who seeks occasions of fighting, and wantonly draws on himself a challenge; nor is he justified, by saying, that he was dared to the meeting, he was challenged to the field, if the challenge was drawn on him by his own conduct, his own words; if the particular occasion was ridiculous, or his cause unjustifiable. Men may almost secure themselves from quarrels by an uniform propriety of behaviour, by avoiding injurious words, base actions in private life, and perfidious, oppressive politics, in publick. Though duelling (and it is a dangerous concession) may be thus necessary to restrain offences that do not fall under the eye of the law, the occasions should be important, and the man should be one who is free to act for himself, answerable for his own conduct, and accountable to the world and posterity for a share of reputation inherited or acquired. Youths placed at a seat of learning are not free to act for themselves; while they continue there, their honour is obedience to the laws; they are not guardians of their own reputation, they are wards under the governors of the state, to whom their parents have committed them in trust. The magistrates, therefore, are answerable for their conduct and their safety, and bound to prevent the extravagance of youthful passion, and restrain from avenging their own wrongs, men, whose precipitance might find an injury where none was intended, who from want of experience and judgement might be too much alive to feeling, or too intemperate in revenging. The power of the magistrates to perform these duties is at an end; the turbulent and vindictive will avail themselves of the example of their chief; the walls of your city will be sprinkled with blood, and your kingdom become the abode of false honour, the groundless suspicion of injury, the cruel jealousy of reputation, and the sanguinary pique. You were peculiarly culpable, as a recourse to arms was not not necessary to the maintenance of your present, or advancement to a higher rank; you rose to honours and dignities, far too high for your *birth* or *abilities*, without the reputation of courage, perhaps under an imputation of the *contrary quality:* why then was the military renown, which you found unnecessary to the grandeur of your youth, sought as an ornament for your age? Men of advanced age, peaceable professions, tender connections, and exalted stations, may (and it is expected from them to do it) discountenance the practice of duelling; they have already determined their rank in life; they are not now to fight their way through a turbulent, encroaching world; their characters are ascertained; at least the mode of altering them is not *combat*, which will only attract *notice*, raise *clamours*, and be the means of propogating the scandal it was

meant

meant to remove. *Age* will be in itself sufficient to protect men from insults if it be *irreproachable* at present, and if the past years have been given to *virtue,* or, at least, *innocence.* If life has been divided between crimes that claim detestation, and absurdities that awaken contempt ; men, however dignified by *wealth* or *station,* must expect that all who do not depend on their power, or hope from their influence, if serious, will exclaim—if gay, will laugh—if virtuous, will detest. A man whose whole life has been a series of publick injury, publick inability, and publick vanity ; who has uniformly prostituted *mean* abilities to *meaner* purposes ; who employs even the moments of relaxation at his *villa,* when other *tyrants* sleep, when the narrow heart of the *traitor* and the *tool* is somewhat enlarged by pleasure, and the natural depravity disappears in merriment, to *oppress* the *weak,* to hunt the poor, the ignorant, and the friendless from their *dwellings,* by chicane and legal wrong, that he may extend the lawn or grove, and add their little *fields* and *gardens* to the demesne of over-grown, exalted *obscurity* ; who aspired to the dominion of a *learned city,* that he might fill it with his absurdities, villify it by his slanders, subvert it by his corrupt influence, must expect publick hatred, publick reproach, publick contempt, and publick ridicule. In vain shall he display his late-ripened autumnal valour, in vain shall he seek the musick of a good name in the report of a pistol ; he shall find a miserable utility in his absurdi.ies, (which may sometimes divert the publick eye from crimes) and sink to the grave, stung with the ridicule, covered with the disgrace he merits.

CHARIDEMUS.

No. 32.   Monday, February 6, 1775.

Nemo tamen studiis indignum ferre laborem
Cogetur posthac, nectit quicunque canoris
Eloquium vocale modis, laurumque memordit;
Hoc agite, O Juvenes: circumspicit et stimulat vos
Materiamque sibi ducis indulgentia quærit.   Juv.

MC BREACHACH'S DECREE.

A POEM.

NO more shall Grub-street lie neglected, wild,
  Her cellars fireless, and her roofs until'd;
No more her damps the gaunt declaimer chill,
Nor show'rs thro' chinks on hapless bards distill,
Who nought possess but rhyming art, or lungs,
Who deal in scrannel pipes, or flippant tongues,
With equal merit, tho' unequal lot,
To G—l—n, H—w—d, B—l—t, and S—t.

Her

Her ancient empire, o'er Beotia's plains,
Lo! Dullness vindicates, and now regains;
Her chilling mists have sicken'd now the blaze,
Whence orient science pour'd her golden rays;
In fogs invelop'd *Alma*'s turrets fade;
What erst was grand and solid seems a shade.
Her fav'rite son the dusky queen commands,
To lead 'gainst *Alma*'s dome her chosen bands;
Their headlong fury whelms the prostrate walls;
Shanoge Mc Breaghagh rules the captive halls;
Desponding genius weeps, scar'd science flies,
Whilst noise and nonsense mount the vaulted skies;
Victorious Dullness chaunts *Mc Breaghagh*'s fame,
Shanoge Mc Breaghagh, still her darling name.

Behold the chief, his temples crown'd with bay,
Mounts, *Querno-like*, his throne!—asserts his sway!
Obsequious dunces to his levee crowd,
The fawning auditor, the flatt'rer loud:
Ben Saddi here attends with spectrick leer,
And turgid *Fungus* tears the bursting ear;
Whilst each, attentive, hopes a friendly glance,
He views his brother-dunce with eyes askance;
The herd by diff'rent arts allure his smiles,
(For dunces ever most excel in wiles)
Some whine submission, others echoing bray,
Like parish clerks responsive duty pay:
Some with loud nonsense boldly storm his grace,
Whilst others sap with engineer grimace.
His court the chief's glaz'd eyes survey benign,
And bland he thus declares his great design:

"Let

" Let all attend my words with hearts elate,
All smit with love of poesy and prate,
Sworn foes of science, all my bold compeers,
Ye speechers, spouters, mimicks, sonnetteers;
Too long has learning rear'd her haughty throne
In this our isle, and call'd our realm her own;
Too long diffus'd her bright usurping flame,
And chang'd our old possession to a claim:
Since first *Eliza* hurl'd the invasive brand
Which blaz'd up here, and wide illum'd the land,
The foe has tyranniz'd, our efforts vain,
Save the short triumph of *Mc Flecknoe*'s reign.
Now fortune smiles, all hail th' auspicious hour!
Th' expiring embers own our chilling pow'r;
Opposing legions shun th' unequal fight,
And fly, bewilder'd in impervious night;
To me hereditary right insures
This throne—I govern—to obey is yours:
For know (such potent dullness' sage decree)
Mc Flecknoe's spirit transmigrates in me;
Then hear my high behests—The bard whose song
In smoothest numbers only glides along,
Too soft the least emotion to excite,
Quite innocent of thought, verbose and trite,
Flow'ry like brother *Namby Pamby*'s lays,
(Now gathered to the dull of ancient days)
The bard with sock, or buskin ne'er bedight,
Who, shoeless, treads as silent as a sprite,
With motion scarce perceptible who creeps,
Nor stops, but when the yawning reader sleeps;

For

For him shall *Alma*'s choicest honours bloom,
Her laurels crown him, and her bays perfume,
Her captive regifters record his name,
And weekly journals wide diffuse his fame.
Nor empty praises all his scanty meed,
Which nor the naked clothe, nor hungry feed:
No longer shall he friendly night invoke,
To veil his patches with her ebon cloak;
Nor fupperlefs in fmoaking cellars plunge,
Nor, gaunt and weak, in Copper-alley † lounge
But *Alma*'s treafures shall his toil reward,
The chearful draper grafp his ready yard;
Thefe kitchens, cellars, ftores, shall furnish doles,
Beef, pudding, beer, innum'rous pecks of coals:
Thus rags, and fhrivell'd want, shall fade away,
He burnish'd glitter in the blaze of day.
Nor lefs rewards and honours him shall grace,
Who doubly blefs'd with brazen lungs and face,
Fierce as the midnight ruffian, blind and hot,
Out-brawls O'C———r, N—h—m and S———t;
Who the witch, reafon, drowns like mob of old,
With rampant nonfenfe, turgid, rude, and bold;
Who yonder roftrum fhakes with fierce effay,
From morn 'till noon, from noon 'till parting day,
And gains, for endlefs declamation, fame
Which *Henly* erft acquir'd, which now I claim.

" To eternize this throne our arms have won,
That dunce to dunce fucceed, to fire the fon,

Be

† An alley in Dublin where there are many cook-fhops.

Be next our care; left science in the dark
Steal in and fan to flame some latent spark,
Debauch our subjects with her myſtick lore,
And all her rebel exil'd train reſtore:
Let us repreſs her vigilance with guile,
We'll ſeize her armoury in ‡ yonder pile;
And each, a volume's load too weak to brook,
A preface wield, the *phantom* of a book:
Hence bearing ſemblance of our foes array,
As cruiſers hoiſt falſe colours to betray,
We'll take all thoſe, intangled by our art,
Where ſenſe rebellious lurks about the heart.

" Theſe tomes, unnumber'd, reprobate we all,
In one expurgatory liſt they fall;
Againſt our crown they treaſon all contain,
For all betray ſome particles of brain:
Yet we permit (our ſubjects to amuſe)
Light preface-reading, magazines, reviews.

" As wizzard § *Andrews* (learning's general late,)
Had deſtin'd old aſtronomy a ſeat,
From whence the ſleepleſs hag might traverſe ſoon
The various errors of the wand'ring moon;
We from our princely and paternal care,
Not prone to drive the vanquiſh'd to deſpair,
Of ſpecial grace, the dame will entertain;
Our firſt profeſſor be ſagacious *Dean*: †

                                       Yet

---

‡ The Library.
§ Dr. Andrews, the late provoſt, left part of his fortune to build an obſervatory, and endowed a profeſſorſhip of aſtronomy.
† William Dean, Eſq;

Yet rays of favour tho' the witch shall feel,
We banish Newton, Gregory and Keil,
And hug the ‡ book, whose courtly leaves disclose
The arched sky to smirking belles and beaux;
Our patrons all its treasures shall explore,
And Blaquiere understand, and Blaquiere's whore.
And grant, great dulness, tho' my heart be vain,
That here *Mc Breaghagh*'s may successive reign;
Their future kings, *Mc Breaghagh*'s dunces call,
Mc Breaghagh, Pharaoh like, a name for all."

Now let your joys burst forth in grateful peals,
† Clink all your stink-pots, flourish all your flails!

Th' impatient crowd long emulous to praise,
In one full chorus all their voices raise;
Here deep-mouth'd *Fungus* thunders forth applause,
There shrill the sound, from *Saddi*'s fleshless jaws:
Thus some large buck-hound, to the pack the base,
Hears the soho, glad signal of the chase,
Hoarse thunder peals from his capacious throat
The nimble beagle yelps a treble note:
Stink-pots and flails harmonious cadence keep,
As clink the scrape and brush of May-day sweep:
Wide thro' the welkin sings the loud acclaim,
And Grub-street garrets catch *Mc Breaghagh*'s name;
Scar'd eccho screams on Liffey's winding shore,
Long reign *Mc Breaghagh,* Grub-street garrets roar.

‡ The gentleman's and lady's astronomy.
† Vide battle of the Horn-books, Bentley's arms.

※※※※※※※※※※※※※※※※※※※※※※※※

No. 33.   *Wednesday, February* 8, 1775.

Ἵππαρχοι κρεμάσας μαστιγῶσον.

PLUT. in ANT.

TO HIPPARCHUS.

YOU, HIPPARCHUS, have a noble contention with the world, which grows every day more arduous and interesting. You have struggled bravely (and hitherto with success) to produce more baseness and folly, than the world can hatred, contempt, reproach, and ridicule. Yet while your enemies display the absurdity, insolence, and indecency of a late transaction, the labours of your friends to derive it from virtuous motives may not be wholly ineffectual.—We have hitherto been amused by the intricacies of the plot, and the intrigue of the drama: the fable now draws to a denoument. You have avowed the aim of your labours, your arts, your machinations, your oppressions, and your absurdities. You have set your son before the electors of the state. You have said, " behold this boy!—he is by *natural right* your representative;—send him into the great council." The

discerning

discerning partiality of a father may see in his child many attainments, many endowments, many perfections, concealed from vulgar eyes;—he may see superior genius in youthful vivacity, integrity in youthful carelessness, the talents for business in easy manners, and heroick courage in an outrage on the laws, and a violation of decency;—and who would wish to draw a curtain between him and his *discoveries?*—It is with pain we oppose the only scheme of Hipparchus for which, perhaps, he could ever assign a justifiable reason; and were the demand less exorbitant, men might gratify you, for the novelty of your motive. It is the striking feature of your administration to provoke hatred and contempt, by measures unprofitable to *yourself*; nay, by the most odious measures, (which seem recommended to your choice only by their being wicked and ridiculous) you have deliberately overthrown your darling schemes.—This unhappy fatality attends your son; we need only turn our eyes to some *previous measures*, to determine our sentiments of the *candidate* whose cause could make such measures *necessary*.

When we see a wretch, whose native insignificance, inanity, imbecility, and *perpetuity of infancy* might have preserved him *inoffensive*, aspiring to mischief, and exerting his *puny* artifice, malice, and insolence, with a weakness and want of judgment, equal to the wickedness of the attempt, to influence the political opinions, and pervert the judgment of his disciples;

base,

base, bold, and wicked enough to preach and maintain, (with sophistry that would suit the unlettered ages of *Monkish* darkness when *bigots* toiled for *irreligious* tyrants) the most slavish tenets that can debase the tool, and exalt the oppressor; we must trace this conduct to a higher source than his own narrow heart, and find the hand of the *mover* in the motions of the wooden, disjointed puppet.

The office of preceptor, in your state, is a sacred one. The endeavour to pervert and debase it, is treason against the city you govern. To the preceptor, the father of a student commits the morals, honour, and future fame of his child;—he consigns to his care a mind tender, pliable, susceptible of good and evil, in hopes of his marking it with good:—and cursed be the wretch who would stain it with evil, and insinuate opinions which only a villain would wish, a fool would attempt to establish, where the honesty of youth dictates, and a liberal education confirms generous sentiments. To deceive the father, and blast his hopes, by depraving the judgment of the disciple, and filling his mind with false, ridiculous, scandalous, and slavish tenets, is a cruel breach of faith and trust, an equal violation of honour and honesty. You have treated many of your subjects with indecent petulance and brutal peevishness. They are not the airs of *mock* greatness, the magisterial haughtiness, the peremptory tone, the broad stare of confident superiority, the malignant eye, and the insolence of office, that can

can awe the spirits you must encounter. A litte art, a little forbearance, a little moderation, a little common sense, might have influenced many;—do not again venture to confront your most respectable subjects with their slaves;—do not dare again to chide *men*, as if they were boys at school;—the goad of a *driver* must be pointed with steel, not lead. You appear, indeed, like the statue of justice, described by some writer, with the purse and the sword. The accumulation of employments in the state, and the profitable priesthood you have bestowed on the *religious* director of your *conscience*, shew what your friends and instruments may hope. Your excluding the refractory from *offices*, your *indignities* to individuals, and, perhaps, your *interposing* in the disposal of *students* under *preceptors*, will shew what your opponents have to fear. But let not your adherents rely too much on your court influence; *that* will fade as your abilities become generally *known*—and you have now mounted an eminence from whence you may display their *nakedness* to the whole world.

You reproached, you censured, you insulted a number of respectable electors, for assembling to consider calmly a point of general concern—you dispersed their meeting—you calumniated them in print—you displayed the impropriety, the illegality of such debates, while there was yet no actual vacancy. You have committed the very fault you condemned—you have assembled your subjects, proposed a candidate, and canvassed for voices. Surely to prohibit previous deliberati-

ons,

ons, was to confess a wish that the choice might be made without wisdom: the attempt was full of your usual moderation and prudence. You only modestly demanded, that men, independent in their situation, liberal in their sentiments, and respectable in their characters, (many of them of mature age) should resign themselves implicitly to the guidance of a paltry, ministerial tool. When Hipparchus endeavours to obtrude his *son* on the electors, and requests their protection for him, it is their duty to consider whether he deserves it; and weigh his age, past conduct, parentage, connections, and education. Hipparchus has compelled men to a scrutiny which may give pain to a youth of many good qualities, (among which, however, independance can have no place) but the severity is unavoidable, for the enquiry is necessary. The eyes of all men are fixed on the electors of your state; the world expects from them an example of judicious determination, fortitude, and unanimity. Their number is sufficiently large to promise independence; yet small enough to promise deliberate measures, consistency, and concord, without tumult or extravagance. And will *such* constituents send into the great council a boy, without the maturity of judgment and knowledge of men and manners, which are requisite in a framer of laws?—Nothing can make a legislative assembly more contemptible, turbulent, inconsistent, and weak, than crowding it with boys, ignorant, injudicious, assuming, predjudiced and impetuous; except it be

the

the placing along with them *fathers*, vain, weak, corrupt, buftling, forward and unblufhing. Had this young man been educated among your fubjects, they might have imagined, that they did honour to themfelves, while they aggrandized the child of their cares. Had he refided long among them, fo that they might have intimately known his difpotion and character, and proved his virtues; the ridicule of electing a boy, might have been excufed or palliated. This youth has yet made but one ftep in life, and it has been a falfe (at leaft injudicious) one. He has introduced himfelf to the notice of the world, by a defiance of law, order, prudence, decency, and religion, which his fpirited conduct, and the filial piety of his motive cannot wholly extenuate. He has violated the laws of the empire, as a citizen ; of your dominions, as a ftudent ; and of honour, as a gentleman ; and for which of thefe merits fhall men overlook his youth, and appoint him a legiflator ? In your ftate, the offence which he has committed is numbered among the *greater crimes*; there is a peculiar *indecency* in propofing your fon to conftituents whofe laws he has peculiarly violated. The domeftick virtues of this youth are acknowledged univerfally ; but private are often found feperate from publick virtues ; indeed the man who wants both, is a monfter unfit to live ; even *Hipparchus* is awake to all the refpectable tenderneffes of paternal fondnefs. But when a man is offered as a candidate for a *publick* employment, *publick* qualifications draw the attention, and when

determined,

determined, direct the *choice*. The private virtues of *Hipparchides*, far from recommending him to the electors, furnish the strongest arguments against him; his warm feelings, and the goodness of an affectionate heart will make him a slave to his family and connections; his filial piety (which every one must applaud) will render him blind to his father's faults, and dispose him to admire his system of politicks; ensnared by his dutiful disposition, he will be the obsequious creature of parental authority. The publick virtues of the youth are far from being doubtful. What can be expected from the instructions and authority of a father, prostitute in his principles, shackled by his connections? Will he not train up his son to receive the wages of slavery? Has he not now led him forth (after a short lesson of venality) to offer his tender shoulder to the burthens of tyranny? It may be said, this youth has not been fully tried; will you condemn him unheard?—He *has* been fully tried in his father's actions; he *has* been fully heard in the reputation of his father; the whole tenour of his father's life cries loudly, and declares what part the son will act. They are early days yet with the young man. The time for shaking off a parent's authority; the years that promise independence are scarcely arrived. Hereafter, when age has confirmed and expanded his virtues, and given him a knowledge of men and manners, if he can shake off the influence, and forget the example and maxims of a *father*, whose name will be his chief reproach, he may sit in the senate with

with honour to himself, and advantage to his country. Unhappy youth! the conduct of his father will render his first exertions of virtue suspicious; and it will require *many* years of *undeviating* integrity, to gain the publick confidence. The dishonour of his father will hang on him like a cloud; paternal connections will be spread like toils around him, and impede the course of honour; he will go into the great council fettered by promises and obligations, the bondman of a ministry; unable to accomplish the warm virtuous wishes of his heart; unable to indulge his honest feelings, and satisfy his longings after fame; doubly unhappy from his virtuous disposition; unable to be *just* to his *country*, without a *breach* of private *faith* and solemn *engagements*.

You *Hipparchus!* have been as great a benefactor to your children, as to your country. You have given them the example and name of a man, who, since first he heard the name of honour, despised the reality; who, since first he enjoyed power, has employed it in oppression and wrong; and, since first he knew the vain parade of wealth and grandeur, must have also known that it was acquired by the most iniquitous means. A *son* is little indebted to *such* a *father* for dragging him forth to publick *notice*; but you were born to devise and pursue, with elaborate imprudence, schemes for your own confusion. The generous spirit already shewn by the electors might have pointed out to you the catastrophe; yet though you feel the ridicule, the toils, the perplexities, the shame, the reproach, the
anguish

anguish and despair of the situation wherein your ignorance, folly, vanity, and officious venality have placed you; the outlines of tyranny must be filled up; the proper touches and heightenings must be added to give oppression a happy boldness, a due *relief*; and all your strokes (it must be owned) shew a master's hand. All that a rash, intemperate, imprudent, shameless governor could, you have done; and future ages will doubt whether you most *indecently* oppressed, or your subjects nobly *resisted*. You have been overwhelmed with shame and sorrow; and future slaves of government will fear to approach the sanctuary of *learning*, lest (like the Jewish monarch) they should be smitten with the plague of infamy, and turned forth to wander, vile, loathsome, and deserted.

CHARIDEMUS.

No. 34.

No. 34.   *Friday, February* 17, 1775.

Ἵππαρχον κρεμασας μαςιγῶσον.
PLUT. in ANT.

TO HIPPARCHUS.

†YOUR conduct, Hipparchus! becomes every day more surprising, more odious, more contemptible, and yet more interesting to the publick. Your enormities, since your appointment to your present station, have been hitherto confined chiefly

to

† That the reader may the better understand this paper, it is necessary to state the transaction to which it alludes.——On Saturday the 11th of February 1775, some scholars of the college went to the house of Mr. Michael Mills, Printer of the Hibernian Journal, and having inveigled him to his door, under a pretext of treating with him about the disposal of a manuscript, threw him down in the street;—then forcibly carried him away in a hackney coach to the college, holding all the while pistols to his breast.——At the college, after he had been sufficiently kicked and troden upon, he underwent the discipline of the pump, and would probably have lost his life, had he not been rescued by one of the fellows of the university, who seized one of the scholars of the house in the fact; *on whom, however, no censure was passed* by the university.—The provost was under a *necessity* of summoning a board

on

to the police of the state; and men were interested in them only as they were, or hoped to be fathers, and wished to find a respectable and well-regulated place of education for their children. Though some

on this occasion.—By the clearest evidence, Emanuel Thompson, and a young gentleman (the scholar of the house abovementioned) were proved to have been concerned in this daring and brutal outrage.——The provost, nevertheless, would not consent that any censure should be passed on Mr. Thompson, unless the other *(one of his surest voters)* were suffered to escape: —and unless the censure should be conveyed rather against the *injured* than the *offending* party.—Vested as the provost is by that *excellent* prelate archbishop Laud with the most arbitrary powers, the board were *obliged* to obey.——Dr. L—— was desired to put the provost's sentence into *good* Latin;—he *did* it into Latin such as it is: and on Thursday the 16th of February, an Eulogium was pronounced on the conduct of the scholars, in the following terms:

"Cum constet scholarium ignotorum cœtum injuriam admisisse in Typographum quendam *famosum*, nomine *Mills*, qui nefariis flagitiis nobiliora quæque collegii membra in chartis suis lacessiverat;

"Et cum parum regimini collegii cautum sit, ni in auctores et participes violentiæ *utcunque lassos et accensos* animadverteretur; constetque etiam Emanuelem Thompson, illius violentiæ participem fuisse laudando, incitando, et discipulo cuidam scholari obnitendo, qui prædictum *Mills* ab injuriosorum manibus eripere conatus est; visum est præposito et sociis senioribus eundem Emanuelem Thompson admonere, atque admonitionem in album collegii referre."

Of which the following is a *free*, but faithful translation:

"Whereas it appears that some of the scholars of the college have done some *slight* injury to a certain *popular*, and therefore *infamous*

some measures might be traced to your aims, the suspicion of their tendency rested among your subjects, and was too remote to alarm the community. Shameful and open attempts to influence electors *unduly*, and to debase the majesty of the *national assembly*

infamous Printer, of the name of Mills, who in a most flagitious manner had in his Journal for some months past *libelled* some *noble* members of the university (namely the Provost and doctor Forsayeth) by republishing the writings of the one, and simply stating the actions of both:

"And, although the said scholars were highly *laudable* in so doing, and shewed therein a becoming attachment to their *principals*, and that they were fit instruments for the purposes of *party*; yet inasmuch as it is absolutely necessary, (in order to keep up some *shew* of discipline, and to save appearances) that some slight censure should be passed on the persons concerned in said *hasty proceeding*, however they might have been wounded or inflamed by the actions and writings of their principals being thus exhibited to the publick;—and inasmuch as it appears, that Emanuel Thomson was an accessory in *this affair*, by aiding, abetting and assisting the persons engaged therein, and by the opposition which he gave to a scholar who endeavoured to rescue the said Mills:

"Therefore the provost and senior fellows have thought it *prudent* to admonish the said Emanuel Thompson, and to enter the said admonition on the college books."

In this sentence, the provost seems to have followed the example of a clergyman who used always to read the following verse of Scripture in this manner: "And he spake to his sons, saying, saddle me the ass—and they saddled HIM." A poor Printer runs to the provost, and cries, "One of your brutal scholars, last night, dragged me out of my house, beat, abused, and pumped me: Admonish me this Ruffian"—and he admonishes *him*.

assembly by sending thither the unworthy, are great and publick injuries, which must rouse every friend to his country.

An important crisis is at hand, when the people of your state may assert their liberty, or seal themselves bondmen; and as they value their *independence*, they must reject, uniformly, resolutely, and without the least consideration of his merits, every man *whatever* proposed or secretly supported by *their governor*. Your attempt to exert an *undue* and *arbitrary influence* is the fatal blow that would subvert their rights. You have avowed—without shame or hesitation avowed your oppressive and unconstitutional designs;—your act, therefore of *proposing* any man, or attempting, in any shape, to *interfere* with their election, is what should chiefly alarm them; and their utmost vigilance should be directed to your operations.—They will see in your measures an attempt to establish an *hereditary despotism* within their walls, and make their city the *private property* of a vain, ignoble, servile, ambitious, *private* family. Every honest subject in your state wishes to see the crown bestowed, *agreeably* to their laws, on a Native. The only hope of obtaining this darling wish rests on a steady opposition to your aims. Should your people oppose you with spirit, unanimity, and success, the slaves of government will be intimidated, and fear to accept the crown, lest it should prove a crown of glowing steel on

their

their heads. Corrupt ministers will leave this brave people to themselves, and no longer have a reason for sending their creatures among them, when they find the vanity of an attempt to subdue such liberal spirits.

Some of your practices may hereafter appear before the *legiflators* of the land, to your confusion, and the ruin of your hopes. Meanwhile, it is the duty of every citizen to inflict *that infamy* which is the *publick* punishment of *publick* crimes.

The most noxious weeds, *properly applied*, have healing virtues ;—your *wisdom* has found a use for the infamous and abandoned ;—you have called them from the tavern, the gaming-house, and the stews, and set them (in imitation of your masters) to *riot* by *authority* in defence of *administration*. Your instrument in these excesses is an object at which fiends may smile; a man long respectable for his learning and religious life; late in his days, rendered the object of just and general wonder, abhorrence, and contempt; in a perpetual rage ; at war with himself and all the world ; dying, like a *mad hound*, inch by inch. We need but follow the bank to find the spring; an outrage concerted and conducted by *the creature of your creature**, could not be supposed to want

your

* One of the principal actors in the violence offered to Mr. Mills, was a young gentleman supported from his infancy, and educated by Dr. F—s—h.

your encouragement: you have now openly avowed *your share* in the transaction, by extenuating and explaining away the offence, and *supporting* and protecting the *offenders* with all your eloquence, authority, *legal skill, legal subtlety*, legal experience, and political arts. Flushed with your *new* military fame, you were resolved to make all your subjects *heroes*. The head of a *learned state* sat in deep divan with his *trusty* counsellors to plan a *riot*; a *veteran lawyer* employed his important musings, to mature an *assault*. You established your sway by peaceful arts; you were resolved to bring it to its meridian glory by military exploits. You dreamed, you talked of *personal chastisement*, and *manual vengeance*; your attentive courtiers caught the *oraculous* sounds, out-ran their guide, and actually accomplished that of which you but dreamed. But your part in this transaction was still more active, we must conclude, than mere consciousness, connivance, and approbation, from your supporting and protecting the offenders; and when, notwithstanding the efforts of your faithful adherents at the council, one scape goat was necessary to atone for the crime of many, from your turning the form of his reproof into an encomium, inserting therein a justification of his conduct, and in bold defiance of the laws of your state, and of the land, of decency, and humanity, giving a sanction to the most brutal outrage, and publicly exhorting the youths you were called to govern, to the wildest excesses of vindictive cruelty. You laid many schemes before the publick;

lick; the moſt important however were concealed. We little imagined that the *patriotic* idea of a national *militia* was among your projects. You talked much, and with vaſt ſelf-complacency, of diſcipline; we little imagined that you were to improve it by *new evolutions*, borrowed (it ſhould ſeem) from the tribes of *ſavage Indians*. You early explored the treaſures of your ſtate; you ſoon diſcovered that it afforded ſlaves, ſpies, liars, informers, falſe witneſſes, and corrupt judges; you have now found, that it is not barren of ruffians, bravoes, and aſſaſſins. You ſummoned *guardians of your honour* from the brothel; you muſtered your faithful houſhold troops; you ſmiled on them with a pleaſure, which the ſight of *ſuch worth* muſt afford to *ſuch a mind*; you cheared them with your benediction; you ſent them forth to *vindicate* your *name*, with a *valour* ſucceſsful as your *own*; and you prepared for them a kind retreat, under the ſhadow of your *wings*. Riots by *authority*, and public juſtifications of them offered by the governor, in ſhameleſs evaſion of juſt puniſhment, are new things under the ſun. But ſurely the cries of a nation will at laſt be heard; the reverend guardians and inſpectors of the ſtate will repreſent theſe enormous and ruinous offences at the feet of Cæſar; and our juſt and gracious emperor will remove the outrageous and indecent tyrant from the throne he diſhonours. You have ſeverely injured their parents, by *encouraging* in the ſtudents a contempt of law, and a ſpirit of

licentious

licentious cruelty; and every man who wishes well to this kingdom, or desires to bestow a learned and virtuous education on his child, is bound to strain every nerve for your removal. It is, perhaps, an idle labour to search for motives, where absurdity rises on absurdity, as wave on wave; and before we have traced one into its effects, we are alarmed by the rushing of another. You lamented the neglect of discipline, the turbulence, the licentiousness of your subjects; you displayed the cares, the toils of your regency, and plumed yourself in various projects for the *advancement of religion and morality*. Having *hazarded* such assertions, were you resolved to create a veracity for them, and *make* the depravity you had lamented?

You brought forth the *wooden image* of your *Saint* and he was borne about in solemn *procession* on the *shoulders* of men, to work a miracle in the reformation of a sinful people; you founded a plea for the wildest schemes, that ever entered the head of a dreamer, on a spirit of rebellion and riot in your subjects; the charge was refuted, beyond a possibility of credit. Yet unwilling to resign so many goodly *plans*, devised with such labour and exhibited with such self-gratulation, you practised the expedient of artful *sportsmen*, who let loose *wild beasts* by night into their groves and pastures, that they may be hunted down for their *honour* in the morning. Hostile writers set before you the ghastly form of infamy; it was *ever* present,

sent, it glanced above, below, it hovered at your right hand, and embittered the triumph of *successful guilt*. You endeavoured to conjure down the cruel intruder; you *wrote*, you *fought*; the phantom *grew* in stature every moment, and rose more and more dreadful from your efforts. What remained? you called to your aid such *defenders*, as *such* genius, *such* valour, *such* a name deserve, and should ever find. For your refractory subjects you had provided loss of employments, observances, duties, attendances, forms, ceremonies, punctualities, rigours, airs of grandeur, haughty looks, harangues, insults, reprimands, reproaches, accusations, informations, examinations, interrogations, condemnations and censure. For foreign enemies, your respectable champions, your *prætorian cohorts* have prepared *combats*, assaults, stratagems, ambuscade, captivity, outrage, wounds, torture, maim and death. You had *before*, your spies and informers, your tale-bearers and whisperers; the addition of hireling ruffians has compleated the equipage of tyranny. Happy is the oppressor who can command the *harlot* valour of some *ready gladiator*, whose face is against every man, who is eager to strike, on or without any provocation, and whose *obsequious* arm can butcher, without compunction, principle or distinction, in any quarrel.

Evil spirits are said to vanish in a peal of thunder or a cloud of sulphur. The late riot, fostered by your

your smile, atchieved under your auspices, defended by your authority, may be considered as a solemn act of taking *leave*, a notification of your *exit* from the political hemisphere, for you have thereby sealed a formal *resignation* of your influence, and rendered it *impossible* for any of your subjects who retains the *slightest* regard for *decency*, to support an administration, so tyrannical, so outrageous, so shameless, so lawless, so ridiculous, so foolish and so *odious*.

Farewel, Hipparchus! in my addresses to you, I have considered myself as performing a sacrifice to justice. The task was disgusting, though useful. There is no pleasure in tracing little cunning through its windings; in following ambitious folly through its excursions; or repelling the claims of ridiculous vanity. There is no pleasure in marking the failings and the crimes of a weak head, joined with a corrupt heart ;— there is no pleasure in beholding to what a wretched degree of baseness human nature may be depraved ;— there is no pleasure in anatomizing the putrid carcase of a monster.

CHARIDEMUS.

PRANCERIANA.

No 35.   Monday, February 27, 1775.

Proximus ardet Ucalegon.   VIRG.

TO THE CITIZENS OF DUBLIN.

Friends and Countrymen,

IN the resentment you have shewn against, and the serious notice † you have taken of a late *daring outrage*, you have manifested that attention to the publick good, which becomes virtuous, and that regard

† A post assembly having been summoned to meet at the Tholsel, to take into consideration the late dangerous and daring outrage committed by a *party* of the students of Trinity college; the following spirited resolutions were proposed, and *unanimously* agreed to:

RESOLVED, That the late outrage committed by some of the students of Trinity college, on the person of our fellow citizen, Mr. Michael Mills, printer, is a daring attack upon the natural rights of mankind, a violent breach of our laws, and an high affront to the police of this city.

RESOLVED, That as the consequences which may arise from these daring rioters escaping justice are of the most dreadful nature, that the sum of FIFTY POUNDS be offered for the apprehending EMANUEL THOMPSON, a student in Trinity college,

regard to your own welfare, which becomes wife men. May the same spirit animate and direct your counsels on this important occasion. Such an atrocious violation of law and police, considered merely in

college, and one of the principal leaders in the late riot; and that the sum of TWENTY GUINEAS be offered for each and every of the other persons concerned.——[This resolution was rendered useless by an order from the board of aldermen.]

RESOLVED, As the collegiate punishment inflicted on the said Emanuel Thompson (who was convicted before the board of being principally active in the late riot and assault against our fellow citizen, Mr. Mills) amounted only to a slight reprimand for the offence against *the college*; and as the terms in which that reprimand was conveyed, evidently countenanced the crime against the CITY, that a committee be appointed to draw up an address to the visitors of the college, requesting that the proceedings of the board of fellows held on Tuesday the 14th of February, inst. as far as they relate to an outrage against the peace of this city, may be taken into their graces consideration; and that such censure may be passed, and such measures adopted, in the punishment of the offenders, as (by rigour and justice) may preserve order and regularity in the college, deter from future outrages any of the students of the university, and thereby secure domestick peace to the city of Dublin.

RESOLVED, That the thanks of this house be given to the right hon. the lord mayor, for his applying to the provost of Trinity college, to obtain that *right hon. gentleman's* assistance in finding out, by calling over the roll, such of the students under his care as were concerned in the daring and dangerous outrage against the said Mr. Michael Mills, of Capel-street, although his lordship had the mortification to meet a refusal, and that the DISCHARGE of his DUTY in that respect was INEFFECTUAL.

The

in itself, might well deserve your severest animadversion; but the attending circumstances render it an affair of an alarming nature indeed. The national seat of education; that venerable depository where the honesty and virtue of your *children* were placed

The board of aldermen, immediately after the last resolution was carried, sent down the petition of the commons, with the following order annexed to it.

The lord mayor and board of aldermen, considering the outrages lately committed on some citizens, by a body of the students of Trinity college, in conjunction with several other persons, and particularly, one made on the house and person of Michael Mills, Printer, and a freeman of this city, to be of the most dangerous tendency, a most evil example, and an high insult to the police and good government of this city, do hereby offer the sum of *twenty guineas*, as a reward for each and every of the first three persons who shall be hereafter (within three months) discovered, apprehended and prosecuted to conviction for the said riot and assault; and, that a proclamation for this purpose, be forthwith issued; and herein, desire the concurrence of the sheriffs and commons.—In which said resolution, the sheriffs and commons did concur.

A resolution was then made and carried unanimously that the order be printed, and the board agreed.

A motion was then made and carried, that the address to the visitors be read; and it was accordingly read as follows:

To their graces the lord primate and lord archbishop of Dublin, visitors of Trinity college, near Dublin.

May it please your graces,

WE the lord mayor, aldermen, sheriffs, commons and citizens of Dublin, having the highest confidence in your graces wisdom and virtue, and conceiving ourselves to be deeply interested

placed (as it were) in *bank*, to be drawn forth with interest, in due season; that seminary from whence the fond parent hoped to call his child, filled with the generous sentiments, and adorned with the liberal attainments, which fit men for becoming guardians of the lives, properties or morals of their fellow citizens, has sent forth ruffians to astonish the publick and disgrace human nature, by the most savage cruelty. The riot to which I allude wants every circumstance which might palliate, though not excuse such an offence; it was not the outrage of a *moment*; the *insensible unconscious* cruelty of intoxication; it was not the quarrel of a *fellow-student*, where private friendship might have been pleaded; it was a scheme of *cowardly* barbarity, *deliberately* executed by *stratagem* on a *single, peaceable*, defenceless citizen, in the *sobriety of malice*, by a number

rested in whatever may relate to the welfare of our university, not only as members of the community in general, and concerned in the education of the youth of this kingdom, but particularly earnest for the advantage and dignity of that university, having contributed liberally to its original establishment; and our lord mayors having in time past, been its visitors; do hold it incumbent on us, at this time, to entreat your graces interposition to prevent a continuance of the daring outrages of late committed by certain students of the university.

Had we no other object of consideration but the safety of our persons, the laws of the land in which we live would give us sufficient security, by punishing such atrocious offenders with severity; but as we wish to maintain mutual love and harmony between our fellow citizens and the gentlemen of the university, we request your graces will enquire whether some
innovations

number of ruffians *evidently hired* to protect the honour of an *infamous* man, by the terrors of an assassination. Had the crime been punished by those who were enabled to *do so* by their authority, and bound by their duty and their oath, your interposition

innovations have not taken place in the government of the college.

Until very lately her governors were anxious to suppress, and active to punish any misdemeanor of her members; and while the important care of the university was entrusted to a person acquainted with collegiate matters, your graces triennial visitations were rendered almost unnecessary; but, since the direction of the college has fallen into un-academic hands, the irregularity of the students has exceeded all bounds; we therefore most earnestly entreat your graces that, for the preservation of the peace, for the welfare of the kingdom, and for the honour of the university, you will hold a visitation, endeavour to bring to light the causes and abettors of the many outrages committed; and that (let the persons concerned be of what rank or station soever) you will have them *removed*; and that your graces will be pleased to take such other effectual methods as to your wisdoms shall seem meet, to prevent the consequences so much to be dreaded from the present state of the university.

This address was received with unanimity by the house; but the board of aldermen having broke up, it could not then have their concurrence, and was therefore, with the third resolution, postponed.

In a few days after these resolutions were entered into; his grace the archbishop of Dublin (one of the visitors) took his son and another young gentleman of considerable fortune, Mr. St. G——, out of the college, and sent them to Cambridge.

tion had appeared laudable, but not necessary; and the seat of learning had appeared able to support herself, to maintain her own discipline, and preserve the morals of her students. The governor of our seat of learning, by protecting these bravoes of his life guard, publickly avowing his approbation of such outrages, and in mockery of discipline, and contempt of decency, publishing a *libel* on the injured person by way of *punishing the injury*, has destroyed the police and good order of the community; and the licentious and profligate are assured not only of countenance, but rewards from the head of the state; and by paying him *tythe* of their riots, may purchase a full absolution and immunity from peaceful rules, and an eternal jubilee of outrage. Public infamy made vast and daily demands on the scanty credit of a *bankrupt* administration; in such a despair of virtue, such an impetuous, ceaseless *run* of disgraces, this unhappy corrupt man hoped to *silence* those whom he could not *answer*; he resolved to try every thing, catch at every thing, hazard every thing; to establish a band of desperadoes to riot him into credit, and awe the importunate and refractory by the dread of personal violence. The most abandoned of his subjects were lured into the service by the promise of *literary honours*, of the ranks and *degrees* which were *formerly* to be obtained only by a proficiency in their appointed course of study, and they *continue* to fill the community with outrage and disturbance. These wretches have been allowed or rather *commanded* to post up *libels* and threats of outrage

rage and violence on the walls of a learned city; the tyrant sets on his dogs, to hunt the popular electors, that when they turn he may seize them for victims. He hopes, that his creatures may, by insults, irritate his opponents to some act of violence; and with eager malice waits to exert or strain the rigour of the law, and banish them from his dominions; nor will the evil stop here; the example of the governor and the court favourites will soon taint the whole body; the seat of learning will become a seat of war; your streets will be filled with armed rioters; your theatres and places of publick amusement become fields of combat; the inoffensive citizen will be unsafe under his *own* roof; and the innocent virgin under the wing of her parents. The whole kingdom is concerned in the good government and welfare of the national seat of education more deeply than appears at first; even the meanest artizan, the poorest cottager, is interested, as he wishes to find an honest and liberal employer, or an upright and merciful landlord or master, as he wishes to eat his hard-earned morsel in quiet, and find himself safe from brutal outrage: for if our youth be formed, after the example of their governor, to become tyrants and slaves, the consequences must soon be felt through all orders of men; besides, the absurdities and excesses of its *governor*, must bring our place of education into contempt, and cause persons of fortune to send their children to *foreign* seats of learning, to the great injury of the kingdom in the constant drain of money, and destruction of

all

all attachment to their native country in the principal families. Nor muſt you hope to redreſs or prevent theſe miſchiefs; or ſee diſcipline, peace, or juſtice, in the ſociety in queſtion, while it remains under its preſent head. A man, who importuned an *elector* ‡ for his voice, and on a refuſal, impudently *interrogated* him, with the haughtineſs of a judge to a felon, concerning his connections, and the private family affairs of his *father*; and in ſcandalous *avowal* of the moſt illegal and indecent *intrigues*, *noted* down in a *paper*, the reſult of the *examination*. A man, who, when his heart dilated at the convivial moment with the conſciouſneſs of his *merit*, boaſted of having inſulted and reproached your repreſentative; § his ſuperior in age, and, without the leaſt panegyric on the virtue or information of that citizen, infinitely, beyond all degrees of compariſon, his ſuperior in integrity and learning. What diſcipline, or police, can be maintained in a ſtate whoſe governor has openly patronized a riot, and employs a band of *ruffians* to inſult and menace the obnoxious? What peace, while the tyrant and his minions purſue the moſt iniquitous ſchemes, and perſecute with the moſt envenomed rancour all who not only oppoſe but refuſe to concur in their meaſures? What juſtice, when a man of *approved, mature* want of principle, honour, and humanity, armed with very arbitrary power by the
laws

---

‡ Mr. D―――t.

§ Dr. Cl―――t, whom the provoſt boaſted that he had reprimanded for neglecting one day to go to chapel.

laws of the society he governs, has avowed his intentions of influencing an election? Your children will be deprived of inducements to learning; their minds will be perverted with corrupt and slavish principles; and the offices and honours which were appointed as the rewards of merit, will be prostituted, and become incentives to servility, badges of depravity, and wages of dishonour. You are called upon by your own honour, by the love you bear your children, and the duty you owe your country, to rouse yourselves on this occasion. Lay your complaints before the throne; address the viceroy; request, that this corrupt and incapable governor, whose *ignorance* can only be surpassed by his *iniquity*, may be removed from the regency he dishonours.—The appointment of *such* a man, though less alarming in appearance, was more fatal to the kingdom than the most oppressive tax, the most ruinous statute. Taxes can, at worst, but make you *beggars*; and you may have a *hope* of being eased from them by the virtue and wisdom of a future senate. The most pernicious laws can, at worst, but destroy your commerce, and render you unsafe in your persons and properties; and you may have some prospect of their being repealed.—But the appointment of *such* a governor over your *place of education* was intended to involve you in destruction, without hope of remedy—was aimed to cut off the virtue and honour of the rising generation, and their latest posterity, at a blow.

CHARIDEMUS.

No. 36.

No. 36. *Wednesday, March* 1, 1775.

TO VERRES, PROCONSUL OF MACEDON.

THE charge of *folly* may, perhaps, fall on complaints and reproaches addressed to the statesman lost to remorse and shame, who finds in *green* old age the *vigour* of youth to do mischief, without its *honest feelings* to reclaim him. The *phlegm* of your temper, *Verres*, the principled servility, the habitual, veteran depravity, and the hypocritical rigour, may be restrained by the pen of satire, when the pestilence is stayed at the bidding of the physician, or the comet at the voice of the astronomer: yet the useless remonstrances of the present may gratify the curiosity of the future generation, and afford speculation to the philosopher, by shewing what the corrupt governor can inflict and the patient province bear. To render you a more useful engine in the hands of a tyrant, the *prejudices* of education concurred with the *baseness* of nature; and had the path of freedom and virtue been equally profitable, you would (like a true *Cappadocian*) have toiled on in the crooked ways of

servility,

servility, and given a gratuitous support to tyranny. From an ancestor who was the secret enemy of the rights and liberties of his fellow citizens, who conspired to betray the glory and integrity of his country, and stain her with dishonest, dishonourable peace in the midst of conquest, and who was numbered by a nation among the traitors who fought to subvert her religion and her laws, and restore the banished Julian family, you derived hereditary tenets and modes of thinking, which have rendered you corrupt, as well from principle as interest, and entitled you to the smiles of your emperor. A *profound* genius for government is best shewn in the choice of proper ministers and instruments; and never did prince possess this talent in a more eminent degree than *Tiberius Cæsar:* he has learned to despise the *vulgar* requisites of a minister, and discovered that the unprincipled, the libertine, the ignorant, the low-born, the base, and the infamous, will most readily pay that *obedience* which is so necessary to the vigour of government. Our sagacious emperor has honoured with his confidence a set of men, whom princes of less ability would have feared; for he wisely judged, that while from religious and political opinions they were enemies to his family and person, they must from the same cause be the firmest friend to his system of government. Cæsar discovered in you the talents for governing; and never shall Verres disgrace the sagacity of his royal master. You selected for your minister *Calvus*, the centurion, a man whose education was suitable

able to the meanness of his birth, and the humility of his hopes—whose baseness of nature justified the obscurity in which he had long remained—whose share in your favour renders but more signal the contempt he meets with from the rest of the world—whose *pitiful* abilities are calculated in one respect for villainy, as they may render it *unsuspected*, and throw men from their guard—whose prudence is gloomy cunning—whose dignity unsocial malevolence—whose learning dark and crooked machinations—whose reputation vindictive rancour, and whose politicks the petty tricks of a sharking pawnbroker or usurer—a man who enjoys power without being respectable, and while he dispenses dignities and honours, remains base and abject—who is hated and despised even by the people who are led by his arts—who works in secret to disseminate the corruption of his own heart; as some malignant spirit veils himself in *darkness*, while he sends abroad the pestilence. You saw that this man wanted the usual requisites of a minister—learning, eloquence, reputable birth extensive connections, popular manners, and even convivial talents; but you saw in him endowments congenial to your own—retired, sullen artifice, grave austerity, with contempt of decency, gloom, phlegm, avarice, and meanness. Sent to ruin a devoted *province*, resolved to crush the *family pride* of the haughty leaders, you commanded them to fall down and worship, not the *golden image* which the *king* set up, but the *heap of mud* which you moulded with your *own* hands into a shapeless emblem of authority.

thority. In this regular scheme of destruction, the subversion of *Epirus*, the seat of *education*, was a leading branch; and you pursued the *most effectual* means to accomplish it, by your choice of a *tetrarch*.

You fought for a man, the most *eminently disqualified* in the kingdom of Macedon (perhaps in the Roman empire) and you have been *successful* to your utmost wish; you found *Hipparchus*, whose *birth promised* baseness, whose manhood *fulfilled* the promise, whose more advanced years afforded a *supererogation* of iniquity; a man who with a mind *too active* to remain in inoffensive *ignorance*, too *weak* to reason *justly*, gathered from the writings of the *sophists* a *contempt* for the established *worship*, and all that the *Greeks* hold most sacred. Without family honour to be maintained; without the honest pride derived from a virtuous ancestry; with obscurity of birth to render necessary the honours a court can bestow, and vanity to feel their full importance. A man who avowedly *retailed* his infamy, and drove an open, shameless *traffick* with his compliances; a *forestaller* in servility, who while he forsook the venal tribe for *short* and *rare* intervals, merely to *enhance* his *wages*, rendered himself more odious, contemptible and guilty, by an *affectation* of publick spirit. A man who *burlesqued* patriotism, made independence seem fabulous, and rendered virtue *suspicious*, while he supported the cause of his country, only to injure it the more, by raising the *market price*

price of corruption. A blasphemer who pronounced the name of virtue only to insult her, and professed a regard to his country with his *lips*, while his *heart* was far from her. At some happy hour, when *proconsular majesty* was shrouded in the *bailiff's* hut; when your *grave* minion found the reward of his *publick labours* and his *publick virtues* in the *chaste* smiles of an *easy* fair one; and the clemency and christian charity of a *pious, ancient, ceremonious* governor, did not disdain the humble dwelling of female frailty; his three guardian spirits planned the grandeur of Hipparchus. They sat in judgment on his past life; they found it unstained by any trace of good; any scrupulous waverings; any weak deviations into virtue or decency; they set him to rule a seminary, of which he had shown a contempt and hatred by sending his son for education to a foreign land. Yet his conduct has surpassed the most sanguine expectations; and should his endeavours succeed to his wish, the state he governs may soon be fitted for bestowing a proper education *moral* and *martial* on a child of Hipparchus. The first care of Hipparchus was to debase the *priesthood*, by shewing what a depth of malice and iniquity it could afford. He placed at his right hand a man who shames his sacred function, and renders professions of piety *abominable*, by uniting them with those vices which want the palliation of appetite, and are unconnected with goodness of heart, gentleness of nature, and softness of manners. With the assistance of this minister, he searched among the profligate and needy

needy for *spies*; he smiled on them, gave them their lessons, and sent them forth to interrupt or betray the freedom of intercourse, mutual confidence, generous openness, and honest boldness, which should ever prevail among men of letters. To destroy the commerce of affection, which should ever subsist between the teacher and student, he next endeavoured to debase the office of preceptor with practices as infamous and illegal as ever disgraced a follower of the law in a country corporation; and he found one fool, so ambitious to be a villain, so eager to burn his incense before the *leaden* form of Moloch, that he set fire to the temple, and scared the worshippers. His next care was to change the prescriptive disposal of offices, and make employments in the state instruments of oppression, or wages of corruption. An *outrageous* man was by an *outrage* palmed on the people, and violently obtruded (for the most iniquitous purposes) into an employment, which might give him power to harrass the refractory, and exert an undue influence on the electors *officially*. To reward his creatures, intimidate the *scrupulous*, allure the *covetous* and punish the *stubborn*, half his subjects were robbed of the posts, to which in justice and decency they were entitled, that he might reward the *pious* director of his *conscience* with a shameless accumulation of emoluments. To break the spirits of his undutiful subjects; the native petulance which (in hopes of converts) had foamed, champed and curvetted in bridled, enforced, managed civility, soon rushed away

away in *magisterial harangue*, reproach and insult. This man has endeavoured with an unwearied diligence and restless activity, which can *only* be equalled by their *success*, to render himself odious and ridiculous, and injure his country. The profession of an advocate, the government of a considerable state, and the vocation of a ministerial drudge, might afford employment enough to *fill*, and infamy enough to *content* an ordinary mind. The senate-house, the courts of justice, the walls of his own city might afford as many and notable occasions of shewing malevolence, vanity, folly, ignorance, and inability, as a reasonable man could desire; but, the vast *ambition* of *Hipparchus (insatiable* as his *avarice)* grows by *gratification,* and aims at a prodigious portentous *infamy,* before unknown and unconceivable. He thinks his labours too light, the witnesses of his shame too *few*; and finds leisure in the midst of *pleadings* doubly laborious from ignorance of law, ministerial machinations, schemes of reformation, oppression, and persecution, for the polite toils of composition. The *press* too teems with monuments of his *genius* and *virtues*; and he appeals to the whole empire for a certificate of shame. He feared that the *memory* of his *folly* might perish with the schemes it dictated, and immortalized it with *eloquence* all his *own.* His *virtues* however require no such blazon; *their fame* must be lasting as the injuries for which his country is indebted to him. He *studiously* endeavoured to make their seat of education vile in the sight of the people

people by false and malicious insinuations, and he *casually* obtained his desire by the *style* and *composition* of his writings; which (like the writer) unite meanness with an attempt at dignity, and become more vile and contemptible from an affectation of excellence. His schemes and his literary labours had now (as we imagined) fixed the herculean pillars, beyond which it was impossible to find a region of absurdity. We were soon undeceived; when a learned *judge*, from the hallowed *seat of justice*, told us that our ruler was a *public nuisance*, a violator of peace and civil order, a rebel against the laws, an author of guilty example to the rising generation. When we found the man, to whose care the *education* and *protection* of the *youth* of a *nation* was entrusted, like a hot-brained boy proud of his new sword, a *tavern brawler*, a *midnight rioter*, the *bully of a gaming table*, or the *bravo of an harlot*, throwing out menaces of violence, and engaged in a combat (in his own despite) for which nothing could have given him courage, but the tempting prospect of injuring his country, and the alluring intrinsic absurdity of the measure. The *courage* of this man is exactly like his *patriotism*; he hopes to find the reputation of virtue in hypocrisy, and to pass for *hero* by becoming *Ruffian*. The descent of a man who falls into infamy and guilt (like *that* of a body to the earth) is accelerated every moment, Hipparchus not only scandalized and injured the state he was sent to govern, by foolish and pernicious

ous schemes, but shewed himself the base and contemptible *scribbler* in their defence; not sufficiently ridiculous in the character of a *pamphleteer*, this master of surprizes came forth, to the astonishment of the world, a *duellist*; not content with the laurels reaped by his *single arm*, he mustered a band of *rioters*, and sent them to proclaim his *virtues*, by such an *outrage* as is scarcely credible in a civilized, seldom seen in the most barbarous state; and not satisfied with the oblique rays which this affair reflected on him, he set himself in a conspicuous point of view, where its whole lustre converged. He and his minions at the council defended the justice of the action, protected the actors, and forced to yield to a *slight* punishment, one who added to the crime of rioting the sending a challenge; he converted a ceremony intended for the maintenance of discipline into an exhortation to outrage; and instead of an *admonition* to a *rioter*, the subjects of *Hipparchus* heard a *libel* on a peaceable, injured *citizen*, and a panegyrick on riots.

In what a respectable and uncommon light the governor of a learned community appears! Surrounded by his myrmidons, the most unhappy abandoned youths of the state; his pallid countenance, deadly, malicious, and marked with anguish, like that of some *felon* who has just expired on the rack, faintly enlivened with a malignant joy: and his *baneful* eye glaring on the faithful ruffians with the dim, sickly, malignant flame of an unwholsome meteor

From rival wits and witlings fore,
The rhyming prank I long forebore;
The malice of a thankless age
My pinions clipt, restrain'd my rage,
To prose confin'd me for a time,
And brought a sober ebb of rhyme;
But see the maid again attend,
To sing my brother and my friend;
Again the spring-tide wave o'erflows,
With prose in verse—or verse in prose.

A thousand bards thy praise endite,
But I the subject claim, by right;
What bard can celebrate like me
Pursuits in which we both agree?
From Gorge expect the deathless name;
The *proper* poet of thy fame.
Alike our studies and our arts,
With equal genius different hearts,
Our souls with flame congenial glow;
And ah! congenial fates we know.
With equal dignity and praise,
You wear the olive, I the bays;
Alike by cruel Fortune hurl'd,
To buffet with an envious world,
Opprest with injuries and wrongs,
Midst evil days and evil tongues;
While taunting ridicule pursues
'RANCERO's schemes, and Howard's muse,
While merit wakes an envious tribe,
The poet's theme, the witlings gibe.

Both skill'd to rein the manag'd steed;
And both renown'd for warlike deed;
But you with *pistols* take the field,
While I the polish'd *rapier* wield:
You dar'd an author * to the fight,
An author-printer † own'd my might;
Here too the parallel we find;
I dar'd the lame, and you the blind.
Projectors both and mighty planners;
Both men of fine and polish'd manners,
Alike adorn a viceroy's court,
With studied bow and graceful port;
With happy airs with labour'd ease,
And courtly Stanhope's skill to please.
'Tis your's in senate-house to shine,
In meeting of attornies mine.
Both writers of no mean degree,
You prose profess, I poetry;
Behind the maid I boldly ride,
Who sits on Pegasus astride;
While you're content to walk the street,
With her who trudges on her feet.
Both doom'd to wield the luckless pen,
'Midst sland'rous tribes of little men;
You schemes for Alma's youth indite,
I rules for young attornies write.
Criticks in building, planting, writing,
Admir'd for reading, and reciting;

While

---

* Mr. Doyle, who published an address to the electors of the university, in November 1774.

† George Faulkner, printer of the Dublin Journal.

While Alma's sons to speak you train,
I for their use supply the scene.
Soon may thy theatre arise !
Thrice welcome sight to Howard's eyes.
There shall my injur'd muse have room,
And there my heroes find a tomb ;
There shall *Almeyda* tread the stage,
And there my *Rival monarchs* rage ;
There, while a nation crowds to hear,
Shall *you* and *I* the buskin wear ;
You tread the stage you built, my friend !
And I perform the part I penn'd.

   Return we to our parallel,
The points wherein we both excel.
Both boast the sumptuous house, and plate,
The splendid board, the lordly state ;
And each supreme Mecenas fits,
To deal out ivy to the wits.
In *this* I own we disagree,
And blockheads give the palm to me ;
I've somewhat more of legal skill,
And some few honest scruples still ;
While *you*, I must allow perforce,
Are *higher* in Ambition's course ;
Twin brothers of resembling face,
Yet boasting each a separate grace ;
The pleas'd spectator's eye we strike,
With features diff'rent yet alike.
Alas, my brother and my friend !
What cares, what toils thy age attend !

Why, brother, did thy noble zeal
So strongly glow for Alma's weal?
Why would'st thou risque thy ease and fame,
A moody murm'ring race to tame?
To guide their wayward erring voice,
And kindly *over-rule* their choice,
To quell the rebel, votes to seek,
And know the toils of reading Greek.
As when a youngster unaware,
Has mounted on a skittish mare,
While now the vixen starts and prances,
Now kicks, now retrograde advances;
Legs, arms, fatigu'd, and head full addle,
He wishes Satan in the saddle;
Prancer—on Alma's crupper mounted,
For lost by many a fool was counted;
Yet shall—he (though the jade uncivil
Kicks, tears, and plunges, like a devil)
Trot on bespatter'd—but unhurt,
Amidst an atmosphere of dirt;
To NONSENSE—happy province, guide her,
And long and lustily bestride her.——
Or as when cat of mighty soul,
Is set adrift in wooden bowl;
Adrift on stranger element,
In wooden bark is Hely sent;
The element, our seat of learning,—
The wooden bowl his own discerning;
Yet shall he bristle up his tail,
And spit at dogs *that bark and rail.*——

At

At Dionysius' witty court,
(So heav'n ordain'd to make him sport)
There dwelt, of shallow-pated fame,
A courtier—Damocles his name
This man just saw the skin of things,
And thought no mortals blest like kings.
' O what the joy, my liege! (says he)
' To be a monarch great—like thee;
' To sleep on purple, eat in plate,
' And live in luxury and state;
' Thus to be prais'd, and flatter'd still,
' And have a nation at one's will;
' Thousands attending on my leisure;
' Thousands employ'd to give me pleasure.'
The king loll'd out a gibing tongue—
For well he knew the fool was wrong;
And winking to some wags stood nigh;—
' Would you the joys of empire try?
' Well—to the trial I agree—
' Be—for a week—a king like me.
' My crown, my sceptre I resign,
' My throne—my guards, they all are thine.'—
When kings command—'tis said and done.——
Lo!—Damocles upon the throne.—
As big he look'd as Dublin's may'r,
Or Hely in the provost's chair.
Sicilia's youth to read he teaches,
He summon'd boards, he utter'd speeches,
He altered laws, he publish'd books,
And dealt preferment in his looks;

He

He speaks—and lecturers are chairs;
He nods—lo! *Sicily* at prayers.
He had his projects, and disguises,
His hints, his whispers, lies, surmises;
His tools, his flatt'rers, spies and slaves,
Buffoons, informers, liars, *braves*;
And chose a rev'rend calm adviser,
A pious priest, to make him wiser.
With flatt'ry ply'd from morn to noon,
He griev'd his reign must end so soon.
Oh, what the transports monarchs prove.——
Bless me!—what's that I see above?
(For o'er him by a single hair,
That trembl'd at each breath of air,
A sword as vast and weighty hung,
As e'er at belt of giant swung)
' If this be empire—faith! I'll none;
' Pluto for me may fill the throne.—
' Take, Sir, I beg you—take your pain—
' Your sceptre and your sword again.
' No more their pomp to kings I grudge;
' Make me a bishop, or a judge.'

No Damocles, my friend art thou,
That,—even thy enemies allow:
No meddling, vain, officious fool,
Betray'd by ignorance, to rule,
And venture rashly on a throne,
Its duties and its cares unknown.
No—'twas no little love of self,
No thirst for grandeur, pow'r, and pelf,

No paltry, ministerial end,
That made thee wish to reign, my friend!
But 'twas thy love for *speaking, writing,
Devotion, horsemanship*, and *fighting*.
And never shalt thou shun the pains,
The toils that wait on him who reigns;
Ne'er of thy talents Alma cheat,
But for thy country's sake be great.——

Yet should thy weary age desire,
To place of slumber to retire,
Should'st thou unfinish'd schemes resign,
And on the seat of justice shine;
With equal genius, equal knowledge,
Shall I succeed and rule the college.
Yes in your place shall Gorgy shine,
Successor by a right divine,
Your brother and adopted son,
To end what you've so well begun.
Who can so well compleat your aims?
As one who glows with kindred flames.
Who can a birth-day speech reward
Like me, an ancient birth-day bard?——
I'll train the youth in glory's road,
To pen, not only speech but ode;
Strains that a viceroy's ear may fill,
Or through a full rotunda thrill.——
Farewel—my chairmen wait below,
This moment I'll to levee go,
To crave at old Sir Simon's hand,
A trifling, but a just demand;

That

That when you gain the chancellor's mace,
I may be provost in your place.
Engrafted thus on Alma's name,
Together shall we spring to fame;
As crab and medlar scions grow,
Like brothers on one apple-bough.
Or as twin bladders puff'd with wind,
By truant school-boy left behind,
Together held by packthread bond,
Sail with the stream in union fond,
So Gorge and Hely, side by side,
Shall down the tide of glory ride.

G. E. H.

No. 38.

No. 38.   *Wednesday, March 8, 1775.*

*Me, naked me, to posts, to pumps they draw,
To shame eternal, or eternal law.*   POPE.

THE Editor is extremely concerned at his being unable to gratify the curiosity of the Publick with the remainder of the authentick and entertaining memoirs of *Mrs. College* *, as the copy was, by an unlucky mistake, sold to a pastry cook or tobacconist, along with some rheams of a history of Ireland. He has, however, commenced a diligent search through the pastry and snuff shops, in hopes of recovering the copy; and earnestly requests, that gentlemen who find Fragments of this Work in envelopes of any commodity, will send them to the chambers of the Editor, No. 64, at the old side of the *new* or HARCOURT square in Trinity college, that they may appear in a 2d Edition. —The Contents of a few Chapters were preserved, and are here subjoined.

C H A P.

* See the first Chap. of these Memoirs, No. 29.

CHAP. II.

Jack Prance's quarrel with Sir *Gregory Goosequill*, and the causes of it—Sir *Gregory* sends a challenge to *Jack*, who (in imitation of *Cato's* reading the *Phædon* of Plato before he killed himself) reads *Fletcher's* Comedy of the LITTLE FRENCH LAWYER, on the night preceding the combat.

CHAP. III.

Bezaleel Blackletter the Printer, and a set of unlucky boys, amuse themselves with throwing the sun on Jack from a mirror—Jack breaks his nose against *Bezaleel's* rubrick-post, and vows revenge—Doctor *Pomposo*, ever obsequious to the wishes of his friends, puts on a green apron, goes disguised like a sausage-man, with a basket on his shoulder, and sells poisoned black-puddings to the Printer.

CHAP. IV.

This scheme of well-concerted vengeance miscarries, by a cat's unluckily eating the puddings—and Jack disappointed in his attempt, resolves to add the lion's fang to the fox's tail—He hires a mob to seize the offender, and proves to them the justice, legality

legality and humanity of the undertaking, in a most eloquent harangue.

CHAP. V.

The cavalcade sets out on this grand enterprize—it is joined by doctor *Dilemma* and *Billy Slabberingbib*, disguised like chimney-sweepers, and doctor *Pomposo* in the habit of a news-hawker—all stratagems in war are lawful; *Bezaleel* is seized, carried off in triumph, arraigned, condemned, and sentenced to the discipline of the Pump.

CHAP. VI.

The ceremony of pumping described, with a historical dissertion on it's antiquity and origin, by doctor Pomposo—*Bezaleel* is solemnly tried, condemned and *admonished* * for *wasting* the water of the school, by being pumped.

CHAP. VII.

JACK PRANCE becomes universally odious and contemptible—*Justice Bookworm* † recommends it

to

---

* An old joker, who in all the ballads and jest books of those times is called *Black Phil*, being told that Jack had admonished *Blackletter*, on account of his being pumped, " Well! Well! says he, let him take care of himself; if he should throw any more reflections upon *Prance*, he will certainly expel him."

† If we may credit the histories of those times, there did not subsist any very cordial affection between Jack and this gentleman.

to the grand-jury at the quarter-sessions, to *present* him as a *nuisance*—and *Jack* vows he'll get a vote passed against him in *vestry*—The people petition the *royal inspectors* of the school to remove Jack—They make answer, that the school stinks in the noses of the people; that they will *visit* it immediately, and set all things to rights—All the nobility and gentry *remove* their sons from the school, and send them to foreign countries—*Jack Prance*, defeated in all his schemes, particularly in his favourite one of procuring his son Dicky to be elected one of the monitors of the school, *hangs* himself—Doctor *Dilemma*, after studying the speech of *Anthony* on Cæsar, pronounces his funeral oration—The boys make a great bonefire—Doctor *Allworthy*, one of the oldest ushers of the school, a man of the most amiable character, and of profound learning, particularly

man. Being asked whether he had read a panegyrick which Jack had written on himself (full of bad English and Prancerisms) called the *Complete Schoolmaster*, or *Child's Guide*; Aye, aye, says Bookworm, I have; really his friends ought to be very careful of him; the poor gentleman has got a flying gout about him—they ought to endeavour to keep it in his feet.—A young gentleman of the bar having spoken somewhat longer than usual before the same justice, he told the barrister, after the rising of the court, that he was glad to see him appear to such advantage; but having had a regard for his father, he would venture to give him a little advice—" Never, my good friend, make long speeches; it has indeed done well enough with H——n (a nickname that Jack went by) but you see how miserably it has succeeded with Fedy F——d.

ticularly in the mathematical branches, is appointed master of the school—Universal rejoicings throughout the kingdom on the news being spread that Jack Prance had put an end to himself—The school restored to its former reputation—and all the gentry bring back their children.

FINIS.

www.ingramcontent.com/pod-product-compliance
Lightning Source LLC
Chambersburg PA
CBHW032149230426
43672CB00011B/2500